GODLY WOMEN
⟡ *Waiting for* ⟡
GODLLY MEN

Learning God's Desire for Your Sex Life,
Before, During and After Marriage

HONEY GILMER

WESTBOW
PRESS*
A DIVISION OF THOMAS NELSON
& ZONDERVAN

WestBow Press books may be ordered through booksellers or by contacting:

WestBow Press
A Division of Thomas Nelson & Zondervan
1663 Liberty Drive
Bloomington, IN 47403
www.westbowpress.com
1 (866) 928-1240

ISBN: 978-1-5127-2967-2 (sc)
ISBN: 978-1-5127-2968-9 (hc)
ISBN: 978-1-5127-2966-5 (e)

Library of Congress Control Number: 2016901828

Print information available on the last page.

WestBow Press rev. date: 02/01/2016

CONTENTS

Preface.. vii

Acknowledgments..xi

Chapter 1   Staring into the Rearview Mirror: A Wreck
Waiting to Happen... 1

Chapter 2   Still Looking in the Rearview Mirror: Making
Bad Choices...17

Chapter 3   Looking in the Sideview Mirror: Taking the
Path of the World... 36

Chapter 4   Adjusting the Rearview Mirror and Looking
Ahead: Finding a New Path.................................... 56

Chapter 5   Eyes on the Road: Which Road? Finding a New
Life as a Christian 66

Chapter 6   Eyes on the Road: To Date or Not to Date?.................. 80

Chapter 7   Eyes on the Road: How to Stay Busy as a Single,
Celibate, Christian Mother.................................... 85

Chapter 8   Glancing Back for Too Long: Sliding into the Ditch ... 88

Chapter 9   Eyes on the Road: Ways God Came Through for Me .. 92

I Should Have Died 92

God Gave Me Strength.. 93

Meeting Mr. Right! 94

Courting Lessons 101 96

PREFACE

If you've picked up this book, you're probably wondering how you can let me know that the title is misspelled. A *godly* man is a man who seeks the Lord and submits to His will. But there are many men in sheep's clothing who know Scripture. You have to take a longer look—maybe a second look—to see the deception, just as you have to take a longer look—maybe even a second look—to see the misspelling in the word *godlly*. Thank you, Annemarie Bolatto, for helping me with this title.

Okay, so why am I writing this book? Whether you are a virgin thinking of sleeping with your boyfriend, or you are divorced and sexually active, I've been there, and my heart *hurts* for you. I'm not going to sugarcoat this, because God delivers His message right where you live, and I must do the same. I'm not going to dance around hard issues, even at the risk of exposing things that I'd rather not talk about. The night I came to Christ, my prayer was that my pain not be wasted. If one person can gain one "aha moment," my pain will have been suffered for a good cause. Thus, I must delve into my past and share it with you, the godly woman who has picked up this book. My prayer is that as you read my story and share my experiences, good and bad, you will see the lessons I learned and learn from them also!

My heart is for all women, but I have a special empathy for those who have gone through divorce or even a breakup after living with someone. I was not a Christian when I married the first time, nor during the subsequent divorce. I was not a Christian as I sought love, comfort, and acceptance from the world, but there were times when I wondered what the Bible said about sex *after* marriage. Maybe if I had actually picked up a Bible, I would have read the answer!

Maybe you've picked up this book, wondering if God has a word for you about your sex life outside of marriage. He does. I made all of the mistakes, and I want *you* to read this book and avoid the heartbreak—or at least learn what your next step should be after you've healed. As you'll read later, this book was written as an act of obedience. Maybe it was written for you.

Why am I writing this book *now*? My number one reason is because my mom "graduated" to the Lord in 2006, and this book is not going to be flattering to her. I've respected, honored, and loved her during her lifetime, and I would never have been able to write this book had she been able to pick it up and read it. And the mother who raised me is not the mother who passed from this earth.

My number two reason is because I met my godly man (one *L*), and I truly feel that my mistakes led me through several valleys before climbing into the arms of my wonderful husband. In other words, I can show you what works—and definitely what doesn't!

In this book, I've made the decision to change the names of my family members to protect my children and grandchildren. The issues of divorce don't go away after a few months, years, or even decades, and their happiness means the world to me.

In the upcoming chapters, I'd like to emphasize that I might not have made many of my poor decisions if I had sought counseling. I strongly and urgently advise any child, teenager, mother, or traumatized woman—no matter your age or if you have experienced abuse while growing up—to get counseling before even considering getting married. Most churches have the resources to help in some way. If your church isn't able to help at all, look up Christian counseling resources in your area and make an appointment! Many Christian counselors are in the business of helping and can probably work something out with you financially. Please, do not carry your shame any longer. It's not necessary. Sister, you are loved by a perfect God, even in your own imperfect past. And your past is always less than one minute behind you.

ACKNOWLEDGMENTS

This book is dedicated to my very own godly man. My love, you are such a blessing, and I absolutely know that God brought you to me. He may have had to hit me over the head, but I'm so glad I finally recognized Him in you. You're constantly seeking truth by reading the Bible, and always trying to make the correct decisions based on God's Word. This book would never have been completed without you. Thank you for your heart. Thank you for your generosity. And most of all, thank you for believing in me.

And thank you to all you godly women who encouraged me to take my notes and turn them into a book. From all over the world, you have allowed me into your lives and allowed me a peek into your different cultures. It's widened my understanding of the persecution many of you face daily as Christians and as women. God bless every one of you!

And thank you, Dr. Glenda R. Gloria. You've been a blessing in so many ways. Your spirit is such an inspiration to me. Your sights are constantly on the kingdom. You are soaring in your faith, and I'm awestruck. God bless you!

To my children, you are mentioned last but you are not the least! I was born to be your mother and it's been the driving force of my life. I have regrets in my life, yes. But I will always rejoice in my motherhood. You are loved beyond measure as are *your* children. I pray for your lives and the lives of your step-siblings constantly. May God bless you abundantly and may you learn from my mistakes. I love you all.

CHAPTER 1

Staring into the Rearview Mirror: A Wreck Waiting to Happen

Warning:
For as he thinks within himself, so he is.
—Proverbs 23:7

I remember spending the night at a friend's house when I was thirteen. My friend was a couple of years younger than me, and her brother was in the same grade as I was. He and I were also friends. I loved their parents and being in their home. The whole family treated one another with such respect and love. They were normal, or at least what I considered to be normal. That one night I spent there was *amazing*! We sat around the dinner table and talked. I mean, we really talked! Mrs. Ryan asked questions, even to *me* ... as if what I had to say really mattered. I called her Mama #2 for many years after that night.

I grew sad as the end of my stay neared. Oh, I did not want to go home. Dread rose up within me as the hour approached. My heart was whispering, "No, no, no, no, no." If there was a God, maybe I was praying, or maybe I was begging. "Let something happen! Please, please, please, please."

We lived miles out of town. My stepdad was the manager of a cattle ranch, which meant that he was a glorified ranch hand who got to live on the ranch in a house provided by the owner of the ranch. This house was extremely tiny. It had three small bedrooms, a kitchenette, one bathroom, and a living room. It rested on cinder blocks. But it stood in a huge yard with very large oak trees. I loved that yard.

As Mr. Ryan pulled into the driveway, I hurriedly got out and thanked him, not giving him time to get out and talk to my parents. He glanced at our small home and back to my panicked face, and a look of understanding came over his face. He smiled and slowly backed out of the yard.

I turned and felt my stomach drop. I could hear my parents screaming at each other. I just knew that the second I set foot in the house, their focus would turn to me, and the shouting would turn in my direction. I had had so much fun with the Ryans, and I still had a hard time believing that I had been allowed to spend the night there. I swallowed, hoping I could walk in and make my way to the bedroom I shared with my sister.

Just as I set foot inside the door, I heard a glass shatter in the kitchen. I quietly shut the door and then froze, staring in horror at the sight of my stepdad. I could see the anger smoldering in his eyes.

"Who put the dishes away last?" he shouted, glaring at me. He knew who had done it; I was the only one who did the dishes.

I swallowed hard and tried to breathe. Time stood still. "I did," I answered softly. I looked down at my shoes, my heart bursting. Would I get a whipping? Would he make me get my own switch? Would he grab his belt with the humongous buckle that had left many bruises on my body? What would happen next? I felt I was about to suffocate.

I dared to look up into his angry eyes. He was mad, but not just because he'd opened the cabinet door and a glass had fallen out. He was mad that I had not been home, that I had actually left him. I may have been only thirteen, but I knew jealousy when I saw it.

"Sweep it up," he said calmly, looking into my eyes. His voice held silent promise of something to come later, in the dark.

My heart whispered, "Why, why, why? I *know* other families don't live like this! It must be me. I must be a terrible person." Of course, I *had* to be a terrible person to have a mother who appeared to hate me and a father I just plain didn't understand.

I could tell that my mom was angry by the way she was puffing on her cigarette and staring at me. She stamped out her cigarette, walked over, and handed me the broom. I knew they had been fighting, which was probably why she wasn't saying much. If he was yelling at me, he wasn't yelling at her. I got it.

You've probably already guessed that I grew up in an abusive home. I grew up knowing, or at least strongly suspecting, that somehow I was a noose around my mother's neck. My siblings may disagree (but maybe not) that her anger and unhappiness were directed more toward me than any of them. I was the oldest. More was expected from me, and this meant that more could eventually go wrong. And boy, did it.

My stepdad was a man to be feared. Isn't it so typical to hear about the alcoholic, abusive stepdad? Well, he was. My mother was a carnal Christian who had married an atheist. As an adult who has made many, many mistakes, I understand why they got married. The sex was probably fantastic at least in the beginning. Billy was an attractive man. He was a "bad boy" and the black sheep of his family. He had cockiness and swagger. All my girlfriends thought he was so handsome. But God and Jesus Christ? Yes, we grew up hearing those names—but not in the context of love and sacrifice, that's for sure—from both of my parents.

In 1957 Mom was married to a navy man named Larry. That's about all I know about him except for tidbits I learned later in life. But marriage with Larry must not have met her expectations. She told me she'd wanted a baby but couldn't get pregnant. So perhaps she was bored, or maybe she'd married for all the wrong reasons, but eventually she began having an affair with Rodney. I, of course, wasn't there, but I imagine when she finally became pregnant, the conversation may have gone something like this:

Mom: "Larry, I'm pregnant! I'm so happy. We're going to have a baby!"

Larry: "That's impossible. It can't be mine."

Mom must have felt all the blood drain from her face as she struggled to avoid the truth. "What do you mean, it can't be yours?"

"I'm sterile. I can't have kids."

I'm sure you could have heard a pin drop as his lie of omission met with her lie of fidelity. Ouch. And on top of it, she wasn't in love with Rodney.

So there it was, 1957, the era of Doris Day and *Leave It to Beaver*. Mom always did buck the system, so it was probably not much of a surprise to those who knew her when she decided to keep the baby (me) and give it her husband's last name ... as the divorce went through, of course.

Between talking to my biological father and hearing a few of Mom's stories, I've been able to piece together our story. Larry kicked Mom out with little ado. Rodney found out that she was pregnant and wanted to marry her, but she told him the baby wasn't his. Larry divorced her, and six weeks after I was born, she married Billy, whom she'd known for only two weeks. Just thinking about the physical implications of that makes me hurt for her. Was she so desperate that she married the first charmer who looked at her? She had *just* had a baby. Did they have sex right away? The places my heart wants to go and the questions my head wants to ask have to stop there. I've made my own mistakes and have learned from them. I can only answer for myself.

So I grew up calling Billy "Daddy." I had no clue that anything was amiss. Did I feel like I was different from the other kids? Yes. Did I feel like I was picked on in my family? Yes. Did I suffer from the Cinderella Syndrome? Yes. But still I was just a kid. I believed what I was told, which was that I was the oldest of four children, and that was that.

I grew up with Billy's last name. I have a hard time imagining that any school would go along with hiding a child's name these days. But back in the sixties and seventies, I guess there was no problem. Mom just informed each school that I didn't know my last name was legally different from my siblings' name and that she didn't want me to feel like an outsider, which is almost laughable, because actions speak so much louder than words. Every single one of the thirteen schools I attended was complicit in the cover-up.

Yes, I was clueless. So, if there's any incongruity when I say *dad* or *stepdad*, it's solely because I didn't learn the truth until Mom was forced to tell me at age fourteen. Also, I have two half-brothers and a half-sister that I will always call my brothers and sister. I still struggle today when I talk with them about their father. Do I say *Daddy* or *your dad*? *Billy*?

Mom and Billy moved around a *lot*. I was born at the naval base in San Diego, California, and by the time I was in the third grade, we had moved from there back to Texas for the third and final time. When I was in the seventh grade, I was attending my thirteenth and final school district. We lived on ranches, and I grew up loving the country and cattle, horses, cats, and dogs. As a "tween," I was either riding a horse, reading a book about horses, doing chores as I was thinking about horses, or climbing trees to stare at the horses—where I would also read books about horses.

As you can imagine, after switching from twelve different schools and making new friends over and over again, I was very shy. I mean, what was the point of making friends if I was only going to move again? Little did I know that the reason we moved so often was because my stepdad was either avoiding the law for writing hot checks, or he was on the run for cattle rustling! We kids, of course, had no idea. Needless to say, we were not a church-going family.

My memories of my siblings are mixed. We were not what I would call "close," though we had a very dysfunctional sense of closeness when there was violence in the house. The yelling and screaming, the cries of pain over shattering glass, usually bonded us into a tight circle of gut-wrenching fear. But while we held that flimsy bond, we also fought like cats and dogs. We had no concept of conflict resolution or how to forgive. We grew up only knowing revenge and rejection. I vividly remember one of my younger brothers hitting me over the head with a baseball bat, and my turning around and throwing him through a window! He was fourteen, and I was sixteen.

But we also had some good times growing up in the country. Oh, the memories of the smell of the barns where the show cattle were taken care of; the smell of oats, molasses, and horse's breath; and even the stench of a stall that needed to be cleaned. I'm not sure if anyone *not* raised in the country can truly appreciate these smells, but I love them still. I have memories of grabbing a bucket of oats, catching a horse, climbing on its back and taking off, and feeling the wind in my hair and the muscles of that horse moving beneath my legs. That was my second form of escape. Reading was my first. I'd grab a book and climb a tree where nobody could find me—on the rare occasions when I could sneak away from the housework.

By the time I had reached the eighth grade, it was apparent that my parents were heading for divorce. How they had stayed together for as long as they had was beyond me. The dark memories of my childhood far outweigh the good, I'm afraid. I don't know how many times we kids would be in the backseat, with my parents arguing in the front seat, when all of a sudden Billy would lean over, open the door, and push her out of the moving car! It was terrifying. Of course, we would scream and cry out, "Mommy! I want Mommy! Daddy, go back! Daddy, go back!" We would be screaming as we all turned around and watched her slowly getting up and start staggering, her form getting smaller and smaller as we drove away into the night. We'd drive home with our dad yelling at us to stop crying or he'd throw *us* out of the car next. The thought of being thrown out into a dark, scary night was terrifying. The only sound heard after that threat would be the sound of sniffles as we'd huddle together (seatbelts weren't used much back then). I'll never forget the tear-streaked faces of my sister and brothers, the empty feeling of leaving our mother on the side of the road, and not knowing what was going to happen to us.

Sometime in the wee morning hours, Mom would quietly enter the house. I'm sure she was just hoping to get some sleep, but Billy would be waiting for her. He'd grab her and accuse her of sleeping with other men in order to get a ride home. The accusations were absurd, but it did no good for her to argue, and the beatings would continue. I woke up so many mornings to find my mom gingerly trying to wash her hair without opening the cuts on her head. But they would always make up … *until my story entered their picture.*

While Mom received the majority of the beatings, we kids were also targets. We would never know what was going to set him off. My brothers have their own horror stories of what happened years later, but the stories that I remember were of receiving bruises from belt buckles and welts from belts and switches. Something even sadder, though, was that when Mom lost *her* temper, she took it out on me. She beat, she hit, and she slapped; but mostly she told me that I was crazy. She threatened to take me to a psychiatrist. Silently, I sat there, my head hung in shame as she ranted.

"You're crazy. Do you hear me? You need to see a psychiatrist. They'll put you away!" she screamed with hatred and anger.

I still remember sitting in a chair with my skinny, knobby knees pressing my hands together. But inside my head I was silently begging her to take me to that psychiatrist so that he would tell her that she was the one with the mental problems. Little did she know (or possibly even care) that she was setting me up for what I considered "normal" behavior. There would always be doubt in my mind as to whether or not I really was crazy, not to mention that I would find it normal to be the object of abuse and degradation.

At the beginning of summer break in 1971, my mom had had enough of the fighting with Billy. She told him that she wanted a divorce and was going to move to Kansas City with her brother, My Uncle Bret. She was going to find a job and then come back for us kids. I dearly loved my Uncle Bret and was convinced that this was a step into a better life for all of us.

Before she left, Mom took me aside and promised me that she would come back for us after she found work. I was scared to death, but I was also looking forward to getting away from the violence. She showed me how to wash our clothes and then laid out a menu of meals for me to cook.

Every night during that period, Dad went out to the bars for the night and came home in time to feed the cattle the next morning. I felt a sense of freedom and joy, as there was no school, no fighting, and no parents around at night! It was probably a good thing that we lived in the country. When I think of the mischief we could have indulged in, it's mind-boggling.

One day my sister and I conspired to persuade our dad to let us sleep in his bed, since he was never home. We giggled and thought of it as a huge adventure! What kid doesn't love sleeping in her parents' bed?

Giggling and feeling a little emboldened by the knowledge that my mother wasn't around to tell us no, I approached my Dad, while Stacy, my sister, hung back and watched.

"Daddy, are you coming home tonight?"

He turned and looked at me, not understanding where the questioning was leading. "I don't know. Why?"

I was so innocent that it never dawned on me as to *why* he wasn't coming home. "Me and Stacy want to sleep in your bed tonight!" He hesitated for a second and then said okay. That night we got into our pajamas and scooted into the king-sized bed, feeling like princesses. But during the wee hours of the morning, the bed became a little crowded when another body moved in behind me. It was Daddy! Should I leave? I got up to go to my own bed, but he reached out to grab me and pull me down next to him. He told me it was okay. Stacy didn't wake up, so I gingerly laid back down, very conscious that something wasn't right.

After his breathing became more regular, I scooted closer to my sister, suddenly feeling a bit awkward. I didn't know why. As I kept scooting, he'd draw me back to him, and he spooned with me. My sister ended up slipping out of bed because I kept waking her up with my scooting over and being slid back to his side of the bed. I'm still grateful to this day that she wasn't in the bed, as a year of sexual molestation was about to start.

Finally, after what seemed forever, the big day for my mom's return arrived. I was heartsick, but I was also excited, because I knew that Daddy's weird behavior would stop once we left him and moved to Kansas City.

I'll never forget the seemingly endless abyss I mentally fell into when I saw them kiss as she walked through the door. I knew they were going to reconcile. I was horrified and still dealing with the shame of what he'd done to me. I was torn. Should I tell her and wreck her happiness? Should I keep it a secret and hope that he'd stop? Such decisions no child should have to make, yet I know that every day more children are forced to make them.

But there was also some good news. My mom told me that my uncle Bret and his family had decided to move to our small Texas town. I can't begin to express how much I loved this man. He was such a gentle person. I'd heard tales of some bad things that had happened in his younger life, and I still don't know the whole stories, but I knew that he always had a huge hug for me each and every time I saw him. I knew that he loved me, and that was—and still is—very precious to me.

So I wrestled with the happy knowledge that I'd have my Uncle Bret around, but I also felt a great deal of shame from what had happened to me—in my mother's own bed! I just wanted it to go away.

And of course my young brain was rationalizing: "Maybe this happens to all little girls. Maybe all daddies are like this." I was indeed one confused little girl.

After reconciling with Billy, my mom seemed to get a burst of energy. She was happy, so we kids were happy. One day after I had been out somewhere (probably riding horses), I walked into the house, and lo and behold, my mom had been one busy woman! We had a back room that was more of a storage room where our freezer was. She had completely converted it into a small bedroom for me. I still had to share it with the freezer, but I was so excited! I didn't have a door, and it was right off of the kitchen, but I had my own little cot, and I didn't have to share a bed anymore! Mom was so pleased with herself. I felt so special—until she said, "It was Daddy's idea." And suddenly I felt like I was in a body of water, looking up and knowing I was going to drown.

The very first night of having my own bedroom, my parents had another fight. Instead of going to the couch to sleep, my stepdad ended up in my bedroom, and thus began a pattern. I would lie still and pretend that I was sleeping as the hands started going places no child should know about. Finally, there was the night when it was more than just his hands, and there was pain and blood. Even through this, I still felt the need to pretend I was sleeping. It's amazing how we can try to escape into our own minds as our bodies are being hurt.

Then one night I had the brilliant idea of getting my sister to come and sleep with me. She was excited to be asked, and I was sure I could finally get a good night's sleep. For such a young girl, I had deep, dark circles under my eyes, and I barely ate, as I had such a little appetite. Mom thought I was anemic. (I think that was a standard way of thinking back then.) I was so confused during that time that I seriously considered not ever getting married because I didn't want to have children if daddies did this to them.

But that particular night, with my sister on the outside of the bed providing "protection" in the dark, I heard him come in, and my heart started beating so fast. *Go away, go away*, I kept thinking. But he didn't. I felt him reach over my sister and start fondling me. I was mortified. I was hoping against hope that she wouldn't wake up. Almost thirty years later, Stacy broke down and confessed that he had been touching her too. When I, a grown woman and mother, heard her words, I felt like someone had hit me in the stomach. I had always felt it was my place to protect my brothers and sister. I had failed.

Finally, after losing way too much weight and hardly sleeping, I started slipping out of my bedroom and crawling into bed with Stacy. For some reason, this kept him at bay, at least for a few weeks. I know my mom must have been confused as to why I had quit sleeping in my bed, but she never asked.

Then one night he came into my sister's room, and all I knew was that I had to protect her. I sat up in bed and asked him what he wanted.

No more pretending to be asleep. I was almost fourteen, and this was a moment of reckoning.

"What? What do you want?" I whispered.

He hesitated and then reached down to pick up the cat and gave it to me.

"I was just bringing you the cat. That's all. Good night."

I grabbed the cat and sat there, petting it as I looked up at him. He knew it was not going to happen that night. I lay back down, pulling the cat closer to me for comfort.

I lay there a long time, debating what to do. I had had enough! Then I heard movement from his bedroom. Was he coming back? I panicked. I absolutely couldn't do this anymore. I was past the point of desperation. I needed sleep, and I needed protection. I got out of bed and found my mom, who was sleeping on the couch in the living room. I remember sitting on the edge of couch and leaning over to her ear and whispering, "Tell Daddy to leave me alone." My heart was pounding. I knew this was going to turn all of our lives upside down.

She sat up, half asleep and dazed, and said, "What? What did you say?"

I said it again. "Tell Daddy to leave me alone."

"What do you mean? What is he doing to you?"

"He's touching me." By now I was crying.

"Where?" she demanded. I could see the anger starting to build, and I didn't know who, for sure, she was angry with.

I gulped. "In private places."

"Has he had sex with you?" Her voice was quivering and low.

"I don't know. He's tried, and there was blood." I was shaking with fear.

I'll never forget the moan that left her body as she bolted off the couch and marched into their bedroom and started throwing things at him, yelling and screaming obscenities. I sat on the couch, crying. But deep down, I was so relieved, so incredibly relieved to have this truth come out.

The look on his face as he came out of his bedroom and headed out the front door will be forever ingrained in my mind. He actually looked at me as if I had betrayed him. After almost a year of abusing me, he was hurt?

After the door slammed I sat on the couch, waiting for whatever came next. Would Mom disown me? I truly didn't know. Would she accuse me of being a home wrecker? I have to say that my mom made a lot of mistakes as a mother and as a woman, but that night she did something right. She hugged me and said, "It's not your fault." She hesitated, not knowing how to proceed. I'm sure that all the years of lying to me were starting to weigh on her. She grabbed a cigarette, and her hands were shaking as she tried to light it. Finally, after inhaling deeply, she said, "There's something you should know. Honey, you've been raised to call him Daddy, and I always believed he loved you as one of his own, but he's not your real daddy."

As startling as that news was, I was so relieved! That meant something was wrong with *him*, and there was nothing wrong with the world. Daddies did not do this to their daughters. Mom also told me that we shouldn't talk about this to anyone except my uncle Bret.

She called him that very night, and despite how late it was, he came over. There was so much pain in his eyes as he hugged me and told me just how much he loved me. I can still remember watching his shoulders sag as he listened to my story. Uncle Bret was a wonderful daddy, not only to his biological children but also to his step-children. He loved his second wife and treated her as respectfully as any husband should. I know that he was having a very hard time processing what had happened. It made no sense to him. But still, it was a "family secret." I accepted this and never told any of my friends, let alone a teacher.

Just after my confession, Mom got a phone call from her best friend's husband, who told her that Billy was cheating with his wife. And if that wasn't enough, Mom received word a few weeks later that Billy had been fired for cattle rustling! They weren't living together, and she had been working double shifts as a waitress to try to get us moved into town. His firing meant that we needed to move immediately. Somehow, she found a two-bedroom house very quickly. My sister and I shared a bedroom with Mom, and my brothers shared the other bedroom. Our world was not only turned upside down, but the pieces were blown away in the storm of lies and deception.

Living "in town" was definitely different. Though it was a small rural town, we were used to being "in the country." So many changes occurred during those first few months, and I was about to finish up my freshman year of high school, so you can add raging teenage hormones to that picture!

Billy moved a couple of hundred miles away with Ruby, my mom's former best friend. I can't imagine how Mom must have struggled mentally, having had all of these events thrown at her in a matter of weeks. Mom was determined to keep a roof over our heads, and she did ... barely. We moved around town few more times before I graduated from high school, usually because she was behind on the rent.

She was also out every night at the local bar. On more than one occasion I had to walk a couple of miles to that bar and drive her home because she was too drunk to drive. It's a sad state when the owner of a bar knows your home number. I will give my mom credit in that she did her best to keep the men in her life out of our lives.

Years later she told me that she had never considered remarrying as long she had daughters in her home. As a mother myself, I completely understand that, and I appreciated her decision. I've tried many times during my soul-searching to try to imagine her life without Christ. It makes perfect sense that she would turn to something or somebody, and she did: alcohol and men.

As mom struggled to get on her feet, there was a short period of time when she had to be on welfare. I can remember her coming home with commodities from the welfare store and dropping them off for us kids to put up as she went off to the bar. I'll never forget the disgusting dried eggs, flour, cereal, and butter. Everything had weevils in it: those creepy, crawling little worms! We had to pick the disgusting, squirming things out before I could make supper. But we also knew we were very lucky to have that food. Otherwise, who knew when we would have eaten!

We kids were pretty much on our own after our move into town. Mom would either leave a note on what I needed to cook for supper, or she'd call from work or the bar. If we needed her, we would call the bar and ask for her. On more than one occasion, I remember the owner of the bar answering, and I'd ask for Mom.

"Anne, your kids are calling."

"Okay," I'd hear her answer from a distance.

And then I'd hear people talking and glasses clinking. I could envision the phone hanging by its cord, swinging slightly as people went past. Usually, after waiting about five minutes, I would just hang up and try to figure out the dilemma on my own. In those days, if I had called back, I would have heard a busy signal until someone remembered to hang up the phone.

One time, though, I sat on the phone for over an hour. I was furious, hurt, humiliated, and angry. I wanted *her* to feel guilty.

Finally, I heard a voice saying, "Hello?" It was the owner.

"I'm still holding for Anne."

"Anne! I need this line. Could you talk to your kid?"

I was the maid and cook. If the house wasn't in good shape, I was grounded. Mowing the yard was also on my list of things to do, in addition to getting good grades and trying to forget events that I wasn't allowed to talk about.

When I became a young mother, Mom confessed to me that she had lived for years with the guilt of what had happened to me. She told me that she had caught Billy looking into the bathroom window one night when I was taking a bath. She mentioned that there had been some other clues too. This confession came on the heels of her joining a church, years after all of her kids had left the nest.

At that time she also apologized for the way she had treated me physically and verbally. I'm sure it was hard for her. My first instinct was to tell her that it was okay, and I did. But as I watched my own children grow up, knowing how protective I felt toward them, the resentment started growing. The depth of the reality that she hadn't protected me started sinking in. I would have to remind myself that I had forgiven her. Forgiveness can be a process, but it *is* easier when forgiveness has been asked for. It's when it's not requested that we struggle with it, isn't it? The harder question, though, was: would I ever be able to forgive *him*?

The truly sad part was that all of this became baggage. I saw myself as "used." I didn't have much to offer, as far as I could tell, so why wouldn't I settle for the first guy who showed me attention after high school? I carried the shame deep within me.

Usually young girls who are sexually abused become promiscuous. I did not (at least by the world's standards), but I carried my shame with me into my marriage. And usually young women who are sexually abused or have witnessed physical abuse in their parents' marriage also marry into that kind of abuse. This I did. It was classic. Needless to say, I had zero self-esteem and had no clue what God-esteem was.

People ask me all the time if my emotions or feelings are *currently* pushed down to a depth that may come pouring out one day because I've never "dealt with" my past. But I believe that I did deal with my past when I accepted Christ. He was my "eraser." Just as there are drug addicts and cigarette smokers who were instantly healed when they accepted Christ as the Lord of their lives, I feel that my brokenness was healed. It's a fact that I was sexually abused. It's a fact that my mother wasn't the greatest mother. I do know she loved me in her own way. Had I already been a child of Christ, maybe I would have sought help during the really bad stuff. Maybe I would have gone to an adult who could have helped. Maybe I would have found counseling. And maybe I wouldn't have made some of the choices I did later in my life. But there was no counseling. These are the facts, and if anybody can learn from my mistakes, then, my sisters, I lay them down before you in total humility and obedience to my Lord so that *you* may learn.

Lesson Learned

Where there is no guidance the people fall, But in abundance of counselors there is victory."

(Proverbs 11:14 NASB).

How amazing is it that I didn't go through counseling and yet I'm writing this book as a sane, whole woman? It's totally, 100 percent God's doing!

In this day and age, we are told by the world that we need to dwell on our past. We need to dig it up, and we need to deal with it. Well, Paul says, "...forgetting what lies behind and reaching forward to what lies ahead, I press on toward the goal for the prize of the upward call of God in Christ Jesus." (Philippians 3:13-14 NASB)

Do I still encourage counseling? Yes, I do! The walk I've walked was tough and could have been less tough … but then I would have a totally different story to tell, wouldn't I?

CHAPTER 2

Still Looking in the Rearview Mirror: Making Bad Choices

Warning:
Do you not know that he who unites himself with a prostitute is one
with her in body?
For it is said, "The two will become one flesh."
—1 Corinthians 6:16

Imagine the Fourth of July in 1976. It was the bicentennial year, and our nation's red, white, and blue colors were everywhere! Flags were flying on every street corner and on cars. It was exciting! There were celebrations in the town park: small booths with gold fish to be won, carnival rides, and much more. And the night was full of promise. I was so excited!

That night, after celebrating all day, I went out with a carload of friends. There was a group of us that went to every rock 'n' roll dance we could find. We were "good" kids. As far as I knew, there were no drugs. Back then the legal drinking age was eighteen, but very seldom did any of us drink.

My heart was bursting with anticipation on this night. I had been accepted at all of my college choices, my loans and grants were set, and I was about to embark on a fun-filled night, dancing to the sounds of my favorite band, The Barons. I don't know if these little country dance halls still exist today, but as teenagers we went dancing almost every weekend. Back in those days, all of the dance halls had one thing in common: every high school had its own little space on the dance floor. There was nothing set in stone, but you always knew where to find your friends, and feuding schools always knew where to go to start fights.

On this particular night, we found our group of friends, and I put my purse down on a table behind them. (Yes, I was very trusting.) Just as I placed my purse on the table, I recognized a guy I'd seen around at a few dances. He was sitting right where I had placed my purse. He grinned and said something offhand, like, "Hey there!" My heart leaped a little as I smiled, but there was a great song playing, and I was going to dance!

That night was such a great night. I loved to dance, and I did! Toward the end of the evening, Joey, the cute guy at the table, came up and asked me to dance a slow song, and my heart started beating so fast. Does anyone remember "Whiter Shade of Pale" by Procol Harum? It was a song meant for slow, slow, slow dancing. So, of course I said yes. I could feel the electricity charge through my body as his hands slowly went around my waist and my arms went around his neck. It was magical. As the end of the evening approached, he walked me to my car and kissed me. I didn't need to be told that it was the Fourth of July. I was experiencing the fireworks! Little did I realize that Satan was getting his first digs into my flesh.

At that time, Joey was still living with his parents. He was nineteen and was working toward becoming a licensed diesel mechanic. We lived about fifty miles apart. There were no cell phones in those days, and long-distance phone calls were very expensive, so we wrote each other letters. We also saw each other as much as possible and became physically intimate on the second date. As the end of the summer drew near and my college career was becoming more of a reality, Joey let me know that he was becoming afraid that I would meet somebody else if I went away to school. I was such a people pleaser and such a doormat—that I decided not to go to college. Instead I decided to attend a business school and become a secretary.

My mom was devastated. I would have been the first person on her side of the family to attend college. As a mother myself, I can understand the depth of disappointment that she must have felt. She was disappointed enough to tell me that I had to move out. I moved in with a girlfriend and her family across the street. Her dad was actually a pastor of a church. What if *he* had set me down and told me that sex outside of marriage was wrong? What if he had spoken to me about who Christ was?

Pretty soon the long-distance relationship was just too much. I dropped out of business school and moved in with Joey's family. All these years later, I have to say that his mother must have wondered what in the world were we thinking. There was no mention of marriage. I slept on the floor in the living room. I had no car, no future, and no hope. And since I had taken on the "legal" name that was on my birth certificate and belonged to my mom's first husband, I also felt I had no identity.

I'll never forget the night Joey hit me for the first time. His parents were sleeping, and he had worked late. When he walked in, he asked what was for dinner. I knew that he was cold and tired from working. I figured he was hoping for a nice hot meal. So when he asked what was for dinner, I had a sympathetic look on my face as I said, "It was only sandwiches." He grabbed me, pulled me outside, and hissed in my face: "So, my mother's cooking isn't good enough for you? You think she should have to cook every night?"

I was shocked at the anger that was directed at me. It was almost disorienting. Who was this person? I tried to pull away and was stunned and horrified when I felt the sting of a slap on my face. The sting of his hand was much more powerful than any time my mother had slapped me. I actually saw stars! I started to black out but didn't.

Immediately he pulled me close and apologized. I kept hearing an inner voice telling me, *Get out of there! You need to go. You always said you would never stay with someone who hit you! Go!* But I didn't. There is something known as *traumatic bonding*. It's when the victim actually ends up comforting the attacker. As the months and years progressed, Joey would hit me, feel horrible, cry, and apologize; and I'd forgive and comfort him … just as my mother had done with Billy. I became great at rationalizing. *If only I hadn't made him jealous. I shouldn't have worn those shorts. I shouldn't have argued. I should have done this. If only, if only, if only …* My favorite irrational thought was, *If only we'd get married, he wouldn't be jealous.*

As time slowly crawled along, I found a decent-paying job as a secretary in the oil field business. I started paying Joey's mom rent. And best of all, I was able to buy a car! It was a 1974 Ford Pinto (yes, the one with the exploding gas tank). But I didn't care. I was so excited to have my own transportation.

Eventually I was able to move into a small camper trailer on land owned by a coworker. I was only a few blocks away from Joey's parents' house, but it was my own place—and I even had a cat!

By this time, my Mom and I were talking again. I had been gone about three years. My brothers and I only saw each other at Thanksgiving and Christmas. My sister had her own hard-earned story, and it involved our mother disowning her for over twenty years, so we went many years without seeing each other.

Long-distance phone charges kept Stacy and me from talking very much, but I visited with my mom about once a month at her office. She got her hair done on Saturdays after work, and if I wanted time with her, I had to visit with her in her office. That sounds really messed-up now, but at the time I didn't consider it abnormal.

Joey and I had a pregnancy scare after being in a relationship for four years, so we figured it was time to go ahead and get married. (I should say, *he* finally decided it was time.) I converted to Catholicism in order to marry him at the altar. (Converted from what, I don't know.) I loved the tradition, the music, and the church itself. But I never went to confession, because something inside of me just did not accept that I had to talk to a priest to confess.

After we sweated over the situation for a couple of months, it turned out that I was not pregnant, but we went ahead and got the rings and set the date to get married. Joey never even actually proposed to me. After purchasing the rings one night after work, we drove to his sister's house and his mom's house and showed them the rings inside the box. He never put the ring on my finger.

At the end of the night I finally asked him if I could put the ring on. He was actually annoyed with the question, but he threw the ring box in my lap and said, "Here." I pulled the ring out and slipped it on my own finger. My heart was hurting that I would never know a romantic proposal, but I accepted it.

Joey bought a trailer house and put it on his parents' land across the driveway from their house. The payments were within our budget, and he felt he needed to be close to his parents, because he and his younger sister were late-in-life babies. Joey was now twenty-three, and I was twenty-two. His mom was still getting around great and was gardening, and she kept an immaculate house. His dad, though, was not doing well. I accepted the idea that there really should be a set of strong hands and arms to help around the place. Plus, Joey promised me that this was temporary and that one day we'd get our own place.

I will say that it was a beautiful Catholic wedding. There were over three hundred people from Joey's side of the family and about six from my side. Maybe that was why I always felt like I had no support. Joey's side was almost like a clan. They tore each other down, but when it was time to party or fight, they knew how to come together!

I'll never forget being at the church and getting ready. As I put my gown on, I have to confess that I had the urge to run and never look back. But where would I go? Who would help me? We had people waiting, and there were so many presents. But worst of all, this would be a horrible way to repay Joey's family for taking me in.

I used to wonder what would have happened if I had not given up all of my friends and one of them had said to me, "Don't do it! Let's get out of here!" What if my mother had used her own past to help me see that my future was going nowhere? But nobody spoke up, and I was too weak. I walked down the aisle, resisting the urge to flee. I told myself that it was just normal wedding jitters. The wedding is still a blur. I remember having a nervous stomach and being afraid to eat anything.

We didn't really have a honeymoon. We stayed in a honeymoon suite at a large Houston hotel that night. They had champagne waiting for us, which was nice for small-town kids. I was a little disappointed that I wasn't a virgin, so there were no jitters about what to expect.

I always thought it would be very nice to be the shy bride, afraid to come out of the bathroom and being coaxed into her husband's arms. But we were way past that! The next day we called friends and hung out at the zoo. Yes, the zoo. We had each taken a week off of work, but Joey said that he needed to work on his mom's car, so we needed to get home. Thus began a marriage that was truly centered on my mother-in-law.

I believed with every ounce of my being that getting married would stop the beatings. You would think that after growing up in my home situation I would know better. Well, only two weeks after our wedding, Joey wanted to go out to eat, but I had already started dinner. After he suggested going out, I looked at the stove and then turned to him and said, "Well, I'm already cooking, so why don't we go ahead and eat here? And besides, I just paid all of the bills for this week. We both get paid on Friday. Why don't we go out then?" He was furious!

I was cooking some meat in a skillet, and he grabbed the skillet and threw it at me. I screamed and ducked as it went flying over my head, grease splattering on me, the floor, and the counters. The meat went flying, and the skillet hit the wall. I was crouching on the floor, crying, when he reached over and grabbed my hair, pulled me to a standing position, and then threw me to the ground.

He began kicking me as he yelled, "Don't you ever tell me how I can spend my money! Do you hear me? Do you hear me? Do you hear me?" Then he kicked me the in the ribs, and I curled up, just wanting to die, because I realized at that moment that I was stuck with him for life and that it had been my own decision. I remember his hand grabbing my hair and pulling me to my feet again. Then he took me into the living room where he threw me across the coffee table. Potted plants and dirt flew everywhere—all over the furniture and carpet, all over me.

He grabbed some dirt, spit in it, and then rubbed my face in it. Then he screamed at me to clean up the mess. There I was, on my knees with spit and dirt all over me. I was so broken, so ashamed and humiliated as I sobbed and tried to pick up the dirt with my hands and put it back into the pots. I was also horrified that I was stuck in a marriage to this monster. How could I leave? Where would I go?

After I got everything cleaned up, he pushed me into the bathroom and forced me to look at myself in the mirror. My face was dirty, with tear stains trailing down my cheeks. He ordered me to take a shower, and then he spit at me again as I got into the shower. To further my humiliation and shame, he would not allow me to close the shower curtain. He stood there and glared at me as I washed off the dirt and the smell of his spit. I believe that at that moment I lost all remaining self-esteem. I know this because that night I went to him and apologized.

That night set the pattern of many fights and many years of abuse. I would make him mad. He would beat me and humiliate me. Then he would expect me to apologize for making him so mad—and to seduce him in order to prove how sorry I was. I was too ashamed to admit to my family that, after two weeks of marriage, I already wanted out.

After two years I found out I was pregnant with our first baby. I remember calling Joey on the phone from the doctor's office. His boss had to call him in to his office.

"Hello?"

I responded, "Hi, Daddy."

I heard a *whoop* from the other end of the line. He was so happy. This unborn child would be born into a marriage that was pretty weak, but we were both excited. Maybe this baby could fix things. Joey would take one look at this baby, maybe with a song, and want to be a good father and husband. Yes, maybe …

And yet we fought during most of that pregnancy. He even accused me of cheating on him, saying that the baby wasn't his. That particular fight escalated to my being kicked in the stomach. There is no fear equal to that of a mother who needs to protect her baby. I lay on the ground, holding my six-months-pregnant tummy, crying and begging God not to let anything happen to this baby.

That fight blew over, but I did remember my mom telling me that usually the best defense is a great offense, and that when you find yourself being accused of something you know you didn't do, the accuser is often the guilty one—especially when the accusations involve infidelity. I guess she, of all people, would know!

When Tony was three and a half, I found out that Joey was cheating on me. He had been going out to the bars a lot. At the time, I was just relieved that the mandatory sex every night was lessening. Let him go! I loved having time alone with my son. He was such a happy little guy. He started off being a mama's boy, but it wasn't very long before he was wanting to walk in Daddy's shoes.

Then one day Tony came inside, crying his little heart out. Immediately I knelt in front of him and tried to find out what had happened. He was crying so hard that he could barely talk.

Just a few hours earlier we had talked about unconditional love. I remember telling him, "No matter what, I will always love you."

Of course, being almost four, he had to test me. "What if I hit somebody?"

My response was, "I would punish you, and I would be very disappointed in you, but I will always love you."

"What if I killed somebody?" His eyes were dancing with mischief.

I smiled and said, "I would visit you in jail." I chuckled and ruffled his hair, and he went out to play while his dad worked on our car. The transformation of that funny little kid going outside and then coming back in so utterly heartbroken killed me.

I kept questioning him, and finally he said that his daddy didn't love him. Talk about timing! It was only an hour or so since we'd had the talk about unconditional love.

I said, "Of course he does! Daddy loves you so much!"

"No, he said that he didn't love bad little boys." Tony was sobbing. His tears had mixed with the dirt on his face and made me feel even more compelled to fix his heartbreak.

This heartbreaking conversation coming right on the heels of our "unconditional love" conversation infuriated me. I marched outside and said, "Did you tell Tony you didn't love him?"

"Yes, I did," Joey responded very matter-of-factly. "He poured nails all over the garage floor. He was bad. I don't love bad little boys."

"You don't just tell a kid that you don't love him because he did something bad!" I was absolutely furious at the knowledge that this man had had my son's heart in his hands and had decided to stomp on it. We started yelling, and the next thing I knew, he was peeling out on our gravel driveway, sending dirt and rocks everywhere, leaving me in a cloud of dust—and a cloud of confusion and hurt.

I stood there in utter amazement. What on earth had just happened? Had we just had a fight about loving our child? I had tears in my eyes, and I could hear Tony inside, crying even harder. I went inside to comfort him and to try to make sense out of this mess.

Then my mother-in-law walked in. She looked at me, almost with glee, and said, "You know he's cheating on you, don't you?" She loved gossip.

The bottom of my world opened up. I was kneeling and holding Tony. I looked over his head and shook my head in denial.

"Well, he is. She's a student at Sam Houston, and she teaches catechism at the church on weekends."

I was floored. Part of me was happy that I now had a way out of the marriage, and part of me was in despair because I suspected I was pregnant.

The next day I found a lawyer. I begged my mother-in-law not to tell Joey that I knew about the infidelity. I wanted all of my ducks in a row when I asked him to leave. Just before my lunch break, as I was about to meet with the lawyer, my phone rang. It was Joey. I don't remember why he wasn't at work that day, but he was at home.

"Is something going on that I need to know about?" He sounded like a little boy about to lose his mommy.

I was dumbfounded. Did he know? I decided to play dumb.

"Why? Did something happen?" I asked.

"Mom just came and took all of my guns. When I asked her what she was doing, she said I'd find out."

I was so angry with my mother-in-law. She knew that this would open up the whole can of worms, and I wasn't ready yet!

"I ... I don't know," I stammered. I remember my finger tapping on the desk as I desperately tried to think of a lie. I couldn't. I was exhausted. It was a deep exhaustion, increased by the knowledge that I was probably pregnant.

"Yes, you do. You know. Tell me what's going on."

"Are you cheating on me?" I blurted out.

There was silence on the other end of the phone.

"We need to talk."

"No, we don't. I'm getting a divorce. I have an appointment with a lawyer. I need out!"

"No! Wait! Seriously, we need to talk first. Please? Please let me talk to you, baby. Please!"

I did what I always did and gave in. I called the lawyer and moved the appointment to the next day. My boss knew what was going on and let me take an extended lunch. I met Joey in a hospital parking lot close to my work.

I honestly can't remember the whole conversation. But he told me her name was Karen and that she was ready to love Tony and was prepared to be his mother. Hell hath no fury like a mother being tossed aside! I won't repeat the words I used to describe what I thought of his offer or of the woman who thought she could come in and take over my child! I was absolutely and 100 percent consumed with fury.

Joey went home, and I went back to work and struggled to get through the rest of the day. After the hour-and-a-half drive home, I walked in, and Joey was sitting with Tony on the couch. I stared at my little boy, gave him a kiss, and went to bed. I slept straight through and didn't wake up until it was time to go to work the next morning.

I kept my appointment with the lawyer and called a friend of Joey's to help him find an apartment. Why was I still trying to help him? I have no idea. Maybe it was guilt and, yes, misplaced compassion. But he was out of our trailer house the very next day.

I was hoping to be able to move the trailer house at some point, but I was pretty much stuck living on his mother's land for the time being. I really didn't want to stay in our home, so close to her.

After a couple of weeks of having Joey beg me to take him back— and with the knowledge that my clothes were no longer fitting and that I *had* to be pregnant—I gave in to the exhaustion of the first trimester. I took him back. I will confess, too, that I was absolutely terrified of being on my own with a four-year-old and a newborn baby. I had no support system unless I quit my job and moved in with my mother. I couldn't do that. So I took Joey back and prayed that the baby would be a girl. I was three months pregnant.

We argued during this pregnancy too. And just like before, there were moments of *Deja vu* when he accused me of having an affair with my boss and when he said that Caroline wasn't his. I don't remember what started the fight, but I remember the look on his face and how his chest was heaving with anger. I'll never forget the feeling of terror as I turned to walk away from him and felt a dish towel being pulled around my neck and tightening in a death grip. I was taken by such surprise that I didn't have a chance to fight back.

As before when I'd been six months pregnant with Tony, I was now about six months pregnant with his sister, and I could feel my baby kicking as I gasped for air and fell to my knees. I grabbed for the towel as I started to lose consciousness. I remember thinking that I couldn't pass out on my stomach. I had to protect the baby. Was it okay? About that time I felt the dish towel loosen in his grasp. I could feel the pain of the air as I gasped and the horrible sound I was making as the air tried to come into my throat. All I could think of was getting air to my baby. Was it okay? A few hours later I felt a kick and a movement, and I heaved a sigh of relief. But something in me absolutely died. I was now in survival mode.

Caroline was born with a virus from a sexually transmitted disease that Karen had given Joey during their illicit time together. My baby girl and I were both on medication when we came home from the hospital. It was just another reminder of how far we were going to have to go to get the trust back. Things calmed down for a period of time, and we were almost happy and were arguing a lot less. I was pouring myself into my kids and was trying to keep my marriage on track. And I was still working full time. But it was almost symbolic that on our tenth anniversary I was alone watching a school play of Tony's—while Joey went to band practice.

We had burned a unity candle at our wedding, and we lit it every year. What should have been a very romantic gesture had become a symbol of such hypocrisy. But that year I burned it by myself, heartsick. Our marriage limped along for one more year. During that time I was beaten, raped, pushed, and almost pushed out of the car; and my self-esteem was sitting at zero. Toward the last few months of our marriage, I had all but quit bathing. It wasn't a conscious thought. I just remember that one day Joey looked at my hair and told me I was disgusting. He was right, and I didn't care.

I was still going to work. I had switched jobs and was working for a well-known software company. I loved my job. I loved the people and the responsibilities I had. I had gone from being a secretary to working in IT. The experience I was gaining was wonderful ... and I was miserable.

One day two coworkers took me to lunch. They told me that it was very apparent how miserable I was and that they were worried that I was sinking into a depression. I considered their words, but by that time, I was numb. I can't imagine any depression medication that would have numbed me as much as my own mind had. These wonderful ladies told me that there was a group of people at work ready to respond if I wanted to leave my husband. On one hand, I was touched that people wanted to help. On the other hand, I was scared to death to bring any of them into my mess. What if someone got hurt?

My heart ached at the thought of uprooting my kids. I was scared to death that I couldn't make it financially on my own. I thanked these wonderful women and told them that I would let them know. I had reached a point where I had nothing left to give to my marriage. There was nothing more my husband could take from me (I thought). I was empty and numb.

The very next morning Joey blew up because I had used the last blank check. He was ranting and raving as I tried to get ready for work. "Who took the last check?" I felt something lightly hit the side of my head, and heard it fall to the ground. I looked down and saw that it was his checkbook. He had driven to the local convenience store, as he did every day, to write a twenty-dollar check, as he also did every day. I never knew what he was doing with the money. Four hundred dollars a month in the early eighties was quite a lot of money. And I had used the last blank check on groceries. He was still yelling as he left the house.

I snapped. It was a Friday, and Joey was playing in his band that night. The building where I worked had a bank in the lobby. I was shaking as I opened my own checking account. I moved most of our money over to it. This is a part of my story where I felt I did what was right. I paid all of our bills for the next two months, because I knew that life would be rocky for both of us. Joey had never paid the bills, and I knew he'd need a chance to get on his feet and to get his mind wrapped around things.

He was playing in a band, so he had a couple of thousand dollars in cash at the house. I ended up with a couple of thousand for myself after paying two months of bills. Now I had to figure out where to live.

The pros for moving to the neighboring town were:

- Tony could stay in his school.

- He would be close to his cousins and grandmother.
- He could stay on his baseball team.

The cons for moving to the neighboring town were:

- Joey could find me and make my life miserable.
- It was ten miles farther to work.
- It was a dying town with no economic growth.
- Shopping would be a good twenty miles away.

The pros for moving to a larger town outside the school district by my job were:

- Joey could stop on his way home and pick up the kids.
- Cops lived in the apartments where I wanted to live.
- It was ten minutes from my job.
- It could be a clean start.

I finally decided to be selfish and move closer to work. Kids were resilient, right? I had gone to thirteen different schools by the seventh grade, and I was okay. My kids would be okay. But yes, it was a selfish, self-destructive decision, and ultimately one that cost me my family.

What was amazing about my workplace was that once I reached out to them, they had everything planned! I was told to go home and start packing. I did just that.

I got home from work and felt so much trepidation. I had hardly ever done anything to cause conflict or confrontation or to draw attention to myself. And I was now about to single-handedly turn four lives completely upside down. My heart was in my throat, and tears burned my eyes, threatening to spill over. I sat down and wrote a good-bye note, telling Joey not to look for me. I told him how much money was in the accounts, that the kids were fine and with me, which bills had been paid, and that I'd contact him soon.

Then I started packing our clothes and gathering toys and personal items. Caroline knew something was up, but she was pretty easygoing. As long as she was with me, she was happy. Tony had baseball practice that day. I remember him bursting through the front door with his glove and that cute cap on his head. He was so excited that he was about to come unglued! His team was going to the playoffs! I saw the excitement in his eyes. I saw the pride. And what did I do? I sat him down and told him we were leaving. From there through the next eight months, I wished I could go back and rewrite this single conversation.

That moment was where I made my first major mistake. I watched the confusion on Tony's face and then the disbelief. He was only eight years old. After I told him, he wanted to go next door to his grandmother's house. I told him no, that he needed to stay with me. I'll never forget that lost look on his face. Never. The tears still well up as I relive this day.

Two friends drove up with an SUV and a pickup truck. I loaded our clothes, toys, two bean bags, and two TVs, and we left. To this day, I still can't believe that my mother-in-law didn't catch me leaving. Hardly anything ever got past her, and there were several vehicles pulled up to carry our stuff.

The kids and I stayed that night at a coworker's house. I called my mom because I knew Joey would be calling her. I didn't tell her where I was, because I didn't want her to have to lie. She was confused because I had never told her about the circumstances I had been living with. She was horrified that I had been living the life that she had lived: the physical abuse, the verbal and physical blows, the rape. I have to say that she was a good support during that time.

I didn't call Joey for a few days. Part of me was scared that he'd talk me into coming back, and part of me was scared that he might try to hurt or even kill me. After I found a lawyer, she chastised me for keeping the kids from Joey. She told me that I had to tell him where I had moved and where his kids were. It makes sense now, but at the time I just wanted to die.

Things actually went a bit smoother than I expected during my phone call to Joey. At the time, of course, he would have agreed to just about anything. He was not doing well at all. I had to tell him pointedly that we were going to get a divorce. I was done. I told him what my terms were for the divorce. We didn't have much. I was willing to take on most of the debt if he'd pay child support. And of course, I got the kids.

We both agreed to share the cost of the lawyer and try to make the divorce amicable. I was so relieved. About a month after leaving him, we did make one last-ditch effort to talk to our priest and try to save the marriage. It was on the day of our eleventh anniversary. But what happened in this meeting was totally unexpected, and I still puzzle over it.

As we were sitting there facing the priest, Joey kept trying to put his arm around my shoulders. I wanted to get as far away from him as I could get, but I was too tired to make the effort. I remember Father Frank looking at both of us and then looking at Joey and telling him to remove his arm from around my shoulders. I'll never forget what he said, because he nailed what I was feeling. He calmly looked at Joey and said, "She's dead inside. You have killed her. She has nothing left to give."

Then he told us that he was not a counselor and that he wouldn't be able to help us. He was a priest! But I think he knew a losing battle when he saw it. We couldn't afford professional counseling. He suggested some books for us, but neither of us read them. I kept remembering Father Frank's words: "You killed her." Yes, I was dead. I wanted nothing from him. All I wanted were my kids.

A Note from My Blog:
Godly Women Waiting for Godlly Men

No Sex? Really, God? But I'm Divorced!

December 8, 2010 at 2:14 a.m.

After eleven years of being married, I went out "into the world" and discovered *real* sex. My husband was my "first," and I didn't have much experience beyond that. No, we did not wait until we were married to have sex. If I had told him no, we would never have been married. (There's something to be learned here, ladies!) There were good and bad things about getting back into the dating world without knowing the truth of the Bible, but they all led to bad!

I truly believed that only virgins were supposed to wait to have sex. I had never picked up the Bible, and I even had the misbegotten notion that the word *fornication* meant cheating on someone. Wow. I could say I was really stupid, but I was just ignorant. I had never sought out the truth. But God had to allow me to go down some really bad, lonely, and even immoral paths in order to *want* to seek out the truth and *learn*! So I learned things the hard way first.

I learned that sex can be *great*! Who would have thought this would be a revelation after years of marriage? But I also learned a few other things the hard way. (I'm very hardheaded.) I learned that if I had sex with a guy the same night I met him, it would *definitely* be a one-night stand. (Duh. Wasn't *that* a no-brainer. I say this while looking back with twenty-twenty vision.) I learned that when a guy didn't call when he said he would, it hurt! I felt used. I learned that if they did want me around, it was only for one thing, and that lasted until something new came along. Most of these conclusions are no-brainers for mature Christian women, but I wasn't a Christian—though I thought I was.

Have you ever glued two pieces of construction paper together? Visualize pasting a piece of pink paper to a piece of blue paper. Let the glue dry. Now pull the pieces of paper apart. You can't? It tears? It also leaves pieces of blue on the pink and pieces of pink on the blue. This represents sex, which is meant for marriage and leaves no tearing or holes. Every time a man and woman have sex, they are "one." If you have a one-night stand, you have just permanently torn a small piece of your soul.

Now, picture yourself taking those same pink and blue pieces and gluing them to other pinks and blues. Try to take them apart. There are now other pink pieces on blue pieces on pink pieces, etc. Get the picture? If you've slept with man after man, and he's slept with a lot of women, that's a lot of tearing and a lot of "pieces" from other women stuck to you in the real world of diseases and the spiritual world of evil. It's the same with sex. We're tearing our souls and leaving pieces that show up in our emotional love tanks: unwanted memories that pop up, unwanted men that pop up, diseases, or even unwanted pregnancies. That's a lot of risk for a few moments of unblessed behavior, isn't it? This is true whether you're a sixteen-year-old virgin or a fifty-five-year-old divorced woman.

God has a wonderful plan for sex. He has a definite and wonderful plan for *you*! I would love it if you would take a pink and a blue piece of construction paper, glue them together in a way that you can see both colors, and then frame it somehow. This would be a definite reminder of God's plans. You could even write a Bible verse on it or below it. Here are some suggestions.

"Or do you not know that he who is joined to a harlot is one body with her? For 'The two,' He says, 'shall become one flesh'" (1 Corinthians 6:16).

"Now the body is not for sexual immorality but for the Lord, and the Lord for the body" (1 Corinthians 6:13b).

"Or do you not know that your body is the temple of the Holy Spirit who is in you, whom you have from God, and you are not your own? For you were bought at a price; therefore glorify God in your body and in your spirit, which are God's" (1 Corinthians 6:19–20).

Be blessed, my sisters, and please place some weight on this advice. It's sent to you with the truest of concerns and love. You are loved by our wonderful Creator. Embrace it and rejoice! God bless!

Lesson Learned

"Now concerning the things about which you wrote, it is good for a man not to touch a woman. But because of immoralities, each man is to have his own wife, and each woman is to have her own husband" (1 Corinthians 7:1–2 NASB).

Joey and I became sexually intimate, which totally blinded me to his faults. He was hotheaded. He was very critical. Both of these character flaws would lead to abuse later. This part is very important, sisters, very important. God knows what He's doing when He gives us rules, when He gives us laws. And He took the time to have them written down to spell them out for us.

Sex is for marriage. Having sex outside of marriage blinds us to the other person's faults. It joins us in a way that's only meant for marriage. Looking back, I *know* that if we had not had sex, we would never have gotten married. It's that simple, and it was that complicated. I also see now that having sex before we were married bound me to him in a way that gave me false hope that marriage would be the answer to run toward instead of the disaster to run away from. And after that I was alone with two small children to worry about.

CHAPTER 3

Looking in the Sideview Mirror: Taking the Path of the World

Warning:
That you abstain from the things sacrificed to idols and from
blood and from things strangled and from fornication; if
you keep yourselves from such things, you will do well.
— Acts 15:29 NASB

This chapter is probably going to be the hardest chapter for me to write. It's never easy when you confront your own sin. *But if putting this out there can change the course of one person's life, if it can stop the heartbreak, if it can pull one sister back to God or plant a seed with His name on I, it's worth it.* I've had to constantly remind myself that I am now a new creature in Christ. I look back at the woman in this story and my heart bleeds.

As I said, I did not know the Lord. During my marriage, I had taken the kids to church, but it was only to try to make myself appear to be a better person than my husband. Maybe I wanted to show the world that I was going to church while he was in bed after playing in the band Friday and Saturday nights.

I believed in something, so I wasn't an atheist. I guess maybe I was more of an agnostic. If we see God as a reflection of our earthly fathers, then I guess it is probably a reasonable assumption that I believed in something, but it was probably too good to be real.

As I became acquainted with my new surroundings and was trying to get the kids settled in day care and school, I dove straight into a loneliness like I'd never known before. One Saturday when the kids were at their dad's, I met a man in the Laundromat, and I became sexually active before my divorce was even final.

The freedom that came to me after having oppressive parents and then an oppressive spouse was overwhelming. It was intoxicating. I could do whatever I wanted. I was *free!* That man wanted a relationship, but I shrugged him off in a hurry. I wanted my freedom!

While I was growing up, my mother kept her affairs hidden from us kids, and I tried to do the same with my own. But I wasn't as successful. I had the misbegotten notion that my mom had been deceptive and that I needed to be more honest. No, they did not meet every man over the next few years—actually they met only a few—but it was a few too many.

To be honest, I was a child in a candy store. I seriously believed that the way to get a man to love me was by having sex. And isn't this the lie that Satan feeds women daily now? I had also lost some weight and was doing aerobics, and I felt good. I felt sexy!

When I look back at that time in my life, I see myself as a pinball with all the little flappers hitting me around, the lights going off as I hit different bumpers that would shoot me somewhere else. I was making no conscious decisions in my divorce, in my life, or with my kids. I was just being thrown every which way by my emotions and the decisions of other people. Every decision I made was based on 100 percent pure emotion.

Forced sex had been a major part of my marriage. Joey had had to have sex every night. I longed for my monthly period just for the break! It didn't matter what time he dragged himself in from work or his Thursday night out with the boys or his Friday and Saturday nights out with the band. He wanted sex no matter how tired I was or how late it was. And if I said no, he would rape me. Yes, it's possible for a married woman to be raped by her husband. To this day, I have a place on my thigh that looks like spider veins to most people, but I will always see the indention of his hand there and remember almost blacking out from the pain. There was literally a hand indention about one eighth of an inch in my skin/muscle—he slapped me that hard.

The constant sexual aggression warped my mind so much that I thought that sex was the most important thing to look for. I needed to find somebody I could please sexually. As I said, my thinking was very warped, and I had no idea who God or Jesus Christ were, let alone what the Bible said of His expectations for me.

In November of that same year, our divorce still wasn't final. For some reason, my lawyer couldn't get the retirement information from Joey's employer. I didn't want the money. I didn't. I told my lawyer I didn't want it. But she wanted to use it as a bargaining chip, and I trusted her. This wound up taking months to get, as his company did their best to hide the information from us. When all was said and done, and they finally produced the paperwork, they showed that he only had a few hundred dollars in his pension after being there for fifteen years.

What I also didn't know was that during this stalling tactic Joey had hired his own lawyer, a lawyer who specialized in custody for fathers. I and my lawyer were both clueless.

Two weeks before Thanksgiving that year, after I'd arrived at work, I received a voice mail from the school nurse stating that Tony had another tummy ache. He had been experiencing them since the beginning of school. We'd been to the doctor and talked with the school counselor, and I was at my wit's end. Remember, there were no cell phones in those days. I could only check my messages at home and at work.

I called the school, and the nurse told me that Joey was already on his way to get Tony. I was a little relieved, because I had already missed quite a bit of work as a result of his tummy aches. Little did I know that the nurse and the counselor had been fed a bunch of lies by Joey's lawyer. It was a setup.

I told the school nurse to tell Joey to go by my apartment to pick up some medicine for Tony's stomach. The doctor had given me a prescription a few days earlier. About an hour later, I called Joey at home and left a voice mail asking how Tony was doing and requesting that he please call me back. I had a growing sense of dread as the day progressed and I got no return phone call.

At about 2:00 I called the day care center to check on Caroline, and they said she was still there. I told them not to let her leave if anybody came by to pick her up. That afternoon as I stopped there to pick her up, I felt a knowledge that something was very, very wrong. I walked into the day care building, and there was no little girl running to me screaming, "Mommy! Mommy!" I pushed the feelings of dread down and asked the nearest day care worker where my daughter was. I knew the answer before she gave it. I was trying my best not to faint as I dimly heard her say, "Her daddy came to get her already." "What?" I responded. "I told you not to let her leave!"

But I was told that since Joey was on the emergency contact list, they were legally bound to let her go with him. I thought I had done the right thing by giving him access to his children. Now I had a hard time concentrating as I drove home to try to call him. But there was still no answer. I was absolutely terrified and confused.

Months earlier my lawyer had asked if Joey would want custody of the kids, and I had laughed. He had never spent time with them! He had watched R-rated shows with cursing and nudity while I was cooking supper—and then yelled at me to come and get the kids out of his way. I had always assumed that the kids and I were just a nuisance to him. I had never expected him to want them full-time.

My one overriding thought during the next few hours was that Tony was miserable with me. He missed his baseball team. How could I have taken him away from that? He missed his grandmother, who had always been there when he got out of school. He missed his cousins, who were like his brothers. At the same time, I did not want my children being brought up by a wifebeater, someone with so much hatred in his heart. I had only wanted to break the cycle of abuse. I didn't want my daughter to be brought up like that, and I didn't want my son to think that his dad's behavior was okay.

I drove to Joey's house, our house, and knocked on the door. It was eerily silent. I went next door to my mother-in-law's. By this time I was shaking, crying, and scared to death. Where were my kids? I banged on her door. I was screaming, "Where are my babies?" She finally opened the door, and I was staring into the barrel of a sawed-off shotgun. There was no sympathy, empathy, or kindness of any kind in her face. Her eyes were cold and dispassionate as she said, "Now you know what it feels like." She pointed the gun straight at me and told me to get off her property.

I was numb with pain and grief as my worst fears were realized. I slowly walked up to the shotgun until I felt the steel of it pressed against my chest. And I begged her to shoot me. The pain I was feeling at the loss of my babies would have been eased by death. She momentarily had a look of pity in her eyes as she told me that the kids were safe. It only lasted a second, however, before she regained her self-control, pushed the barrel at me, and told me to get off her property. I was beaten. I was in shock.

I walked out the driveway and screamed, "Tony! Caroline! Where are you? I love you, babies!" I kept screaming and screaming and crying. I had a total meltdown. I turned in circles, looking all around me. I didn't care if I made a spectacle of myself. Where were my children? I was absolutely, completely devastated. I called out to the God I really didn't think was there to fix this. But there was no answer except my mother-in-law's voice telling me, "Go. I've called the cops. Just go."

Did I get in the car by myself, or did someone help me in? I don't know. Did I start the car and drive home? I must have, but I don't remember. When I got to my apartment, I called my lawyer, and she was blown away. "I thought you said he wouldn't want the kids," she said, almost accusingly. It felt like salt in the wound. But I was so completely "done" that I just answered, "I *know* he doesn't want the kids. He wants to hurt me. He wants to control me. He wants to manipulate me." I asked her how much it would cost for us to have a custody battle, and she told me it would take a minimum of $10,000. I was making around $24,000 a year. Where could I come up with that kind of money? In the early 1990s, that might as well have been $100,000 to me.

That night after getting off the telephone with my lawyer, I didn't know what to do with myself. Have you seen those movies where people are "hearing" their kids' voices or they "hear" conversations in their heads? That night I was hearing Tony saying, "Mom, can I go next door to play? Mom, can I go to the pool?" Or Caroline saying, "Mommy, can you tie my shoe? Have you seen my Barbie?" The voices were so loud that I would have sworn they were in the next room. They were overwhelming. I went into the bathroom and turned on the hot water, hoping that the sound of the squealing pipes would cover the sound of my babies' voices. I turned the water on full force and screamed at the top of my lungs, tears pouring down my face and soaking my clothes. I screamed, and I cried, and I cried, and I cried. I crawled into bed, totally drained. I tried to pray to the God I thought might be there, but nothing happened.

I must have dozed off at some point, because I later woke up in the kitchen. I had never been a sleepwalker, at least not since I was a toddler. But I must have been one that night. I know that I must have been in so much pain that my mind wanted me to end everything. I'll never forget my horror and shock when I woke up in my kitchen with a knife in my hand and the knowledge that I had almost sliced my wrist.

My first thought was that if I killed myself my son would live with guilt for the rest of his life. I knew him well and loved him so much that suicide never entered into my consciousness again. I threw the knife into the sink and started crying once again. With my back against the refrigerator, I slid to the floor and wept. I glanced at the clock, longing for it be daybreak so that I could get out of the apartment. But it was only 2:00 a.m.

I thought about it for a little while. It would be better to do something productive than to worry about going to sleep and what I might do if I did. So I got dressed, drove to work, made some coffee, and buried myself in the work I enjoyed. This would become a pattern for my work life, and I was okay with that. My boss loved what I was doing and didn't mind paying the overtime, thank God. The overtime was the only thing that kept me from having to find a second job, which would more than likely have paid minimum wage.

A few days before Thanksgiving, I was in anguish over not being able to see my kids. But what really upset me was the fact that a wifebeater had my babies. I didn't know what to do. My lawyer casually mentioned to me that in the state of Texas at that time, whoever had possession of the children on the date of the divorce hearing had a 90 percent chance of keeping custody of the child. (It did not matter or make a difference that I had had possession of my children for the last eight months.) So I made a decision to grab my daughter and go to Colorado to spend Thanksgiving with a man I had met there. I had connections through my job with our Denver office and had met a Denver coworker's brother. In my raw, emotional mind, I was hoping to get custody of both children by taking one of them. I did not want to split them up. But the irrationality of this decision still haunts me to this day, because my son was told by his dad, and later by his stepmother, that I didn't want him.

Two days before Thanksgiving, I took some vacation days and called my lawyer. I told her that I was going to get my daughter and take her to Colorado. She told me some things "on the record" and "off the record." All I knew was that I needed to get my daughter, and that would force the courts to give me back my son. I would move back to that town if I needed to, but I wanted my kids back. I went to Joey's house, where I knew my mother-in-law would be watching my daughter. I knew Tony would be in school. I knocked on the door and stood out of view of the window. When she answered the door, I walked past her and grabbed my daughter.

Caroline was screaming, "No, Mommy! No!" She didn't understand what was happening. My mother-in-law was pulling on her and hurting her. My mother-in-law had been through several bouts of cancer. I had donated all of my lunch hours for many years so I could take off work and bring her to the hospital for treatments. I didn't want to hurt her. I took her fingers and unwrapped them from my daughter's leg. I freed my daughter and ran. One detail that always sticks in my mind is that she only had one shoe on. I don't know why that detail stays with me. Caroline calmed down once we were on our way. She asked a lot of questions, and she was in sheer ecstasy when she saw snow for the first time!

When I called my lawyer from Colorado, she told me that our divorce hearing was scheduled for a couple of days after Thanksgiving. During this time I fancied myself in love with the man I had escaped to. Little did I know that he was absolutely horrified at the turns my life had taken and by the commitment that I thought I needed from him. He didn't need the complication, and he surely didn't need legal issues! (Who could blame him?) During my visit he was remote and pretty much just let me explore Colorado by myself. I gradually realized that there was no future for me there. So we can add heartbreak to devastation. I really thought he could fix things for me. What a mess I was!

When I returned to Texas, my daughter and I hid out at a friend's apartment. My lawyer told me there was a warrant out for my arrest. I figured it was for kidnapping, but I was ready to fight for my kids! The warrant, however, was for beating up my mother-in-law! I was so sick of fighting, and even more sick of fighting lies. However, I needed clothes in order to go to court the next day, and they were in my apartment. I borrowed a friend's car and parked in a remote section of the apartments. Then I walked behind the apartments and knocked on my neighbor's door. She told me that cops had been around asking questions about me. I was horrified. I thanked her and snuck into my apartment. I kept the lights off and grabbed some clothes for court the next morning. A friend of mine said she would watch Caroline for me, and I went to court and met my lawyer.

I arrived an hour early so my lawyer and I could talk. We were sitting on a bench just outside of the judge's office. All of a sudden his door opened, and out came Joey, his lawyer, and the judge. My attorney grabbed my arm as I jumped. None of them would meet our eyes. I stared at my lawyer with my mouth open. I was aghast! "What is this all about?" I whispered. For the first time, a deep sense of foreboding was coming over me. It was almost debilitating in its heaviness.

"It's illegal," she answered. "They are not supposed to be meeting the judge without us." She promised to get to the bottom of it, but that part of my life is in such a fog, I honestly can't remember how it was handled.

To this day, driving around that courthouse causes great angst for me. That morning, as we waited for the docket to be read, I remember seeing Joey there for the first time. That was when I was truly scared. He had a smirk on his face, as if he knew something I didn't. Well, he did. The docket was read, and our name wasn't called. I was feeling more and more nervous and scared. As my lawyer and I were talking, a deputy came up to me and asked my name. I confirmed who I was, and he handed me a letter. My lawyer sighed and said, "I was afraid they were going to pull this."

My stomach was upset, and I was scared to death. I asked she meant. The room was starting to spin, and I was terrified that I was going to faint. I looked at her and said, "What is this?" I held the paper out to her. She told me to open it. As I opened it, my lawyer stood next to me and said, "It's a subpoena. They're ordering you to return Caroline by December 5."

My mind was racing. No, no, no! This wasn't the way it was supposed to happen! I was the *mom*! I wanted my kids! No! December 5 was Caroline's birthday! No, no, no, no!" *Return* her? *No*! Who was the one who had gotten up in the middle of the night with my babies every two hours when they were infants—and still had to leave for work by 5:00 a.m.? I was! Who had stayed home with them on the weekends when Joey was off with his band? I had!

Who had cheated in our marriage? Joey! Who had stuck his four-year-old, pajama-clothed son outside on a freezing cold night when there was ice on the ground, just to teach him a lesson? Joey! Who left our six-month-old, cute-as-a-button baby Tony at home alone because he'd forgotten to take him to the babysitter while I was taking Joey's mom for a cancer treatment? Joey!

No! This couldn't be happening! The world had just turned upside down, and nothing made any sense. I was dumbfounded. I was horrified. And you would think that this would have been my lowest point. You would think that this would have been the place where God would meet me. But no, I was stubborn and wasn't on my knees yet.

That night the phone rang, and it was my son. "Hi, baby! How are you?" My heart was racing. It was so good to hear his voice. I missed him so badly. He was crying as he pleaded with me: "Mommy, please let us stay with Daddy. Please don't fight for us." I was bawling. Never had such words torn a mother's heart. At the end of the phone call, I was so torn. What should I do? He was only nine years old. He didn't know what was good for him. Should I actually give up without fighting? Would my children actually be better off without me? Maybe this would give me time to find a rich man, get married, and fight for custody. I was so ashamed. These thoughts are hard to write down, because they show how far out in the world of the flesh that I was living.

The next day I took Caroline to a babysitter instead of her day care. I went to work, and my roommate took me out to lunch. She ate in silence for a few minutes and then finally said, "What would happen if you didn't fight for the kids? Can you afford to fight?" I shook my head. "If you get custody, then you've got this huge lawyer bill. Even with child support, are you going to be able to handle it? I'd have to move out and let them have their bedroom back. How are you going to make it? You can be a good mom without being the primary parent."

I was horrified. Give up my kids? I was also very, very tired. I was very, very broke. Every day I balanced my checkbook, and it was usually under one dollar by the time I got my paycheck. How would I do it? Reality set in. I fell into a huge hole of despair. My heart started going numb as I called my lawyer and told her that I couldn't fight, that my son didn't want to be with me. Caroline was happy wherever she was, and I could provide no proof that Joey had ever lifted a hand against me.

My only hope would have been to show that he was a bad daddy, but if I did that and he was dead set on making me out to be a bad mom, the courts could step in and take them away from both of us. Had he ever beaten the kids? No. He did have some unorthodox methods of punishment, but I couldn't prove it in court. The only witnesses were people in Joey's family, and they were now all against me. I was alone.

I have to say that my mom kept telling me to get mad. She wanted me to feel what was happening so I would fight. But I had fought my whole life. I had been raised with parents fighting and siblings fighting. I had married a wifebeater. I had no fight left in me. I just wanted my kids to be happy. Could they be happy away from me? Would they be okay? Had I been a Christian, I would have known the answer to that.

The next events happened in a blur. I don't necessarily remember the order, because I was living in one huge, dazed heartbreak. I remember standing in front of the judge and giving up custody. I remember him telling me to have Caroline back on December 5, which was her birthday. I remember my knees buckling and my lawyer grabbing me. I remember screaming at the judge that it was her birthday. I turned and looked at my lawyer, pleading with her. "I can't bring her back on her birthday. Please don't make me do that."

I was so weak, I could barely stand. I couldn't remember the last time I had eaten. I had no money. I wouldn't get paid for another week. With the only compassion that this judge had shown during the entire case, he allowed me to bring Caroline back on the following Saturday. I hadn't seen my son in over two weeks. I was broken; I was weak; and I was losing my children. Who was I? What was my purpose, if not to be their mother?

On that same day in court, we finalized the distribution of the material possessions—not that there were any. We lived in a trailer home that was almost paid off. It wasn't considered to be community property, because Joey had bought it in his name the month before we got married. His truck was paid off. I got most of the bills and my car payment, and I was ordered to pay 25 percent of my paycheck to child support.

I was now broke and heartbroken, and still I did not turn to God. I do remember getting home after court and telling God (whoever He was), "I want to make you proud of me. Please don't help me. I want to show you what I can do." I know now, of course, that we see God in the same way we see an earthly father. I actually had never seen the role of a father acted out in my life. You see, it's not that I was an atheist, but I definitely did not have a relationship with Christ. I did not know Him. And I certainly did not trust Him.

That night Joey called me and said, "Now that I have the kids, will you come back to me?" I have to admit that I was tempted. My heart ached for Tony and with the knowledge that I was bringing Caroline back to this man who had betrayed me in every aspect of my life. But how could I honestly be in a marriage where I knew that he could take away my children at any moment, where he could and would always hold them over my head as pawns?

I told him no. I think that surprised him. I believe to this day that he went through all that effort in order to get me back under his thumb, not because he truly wanted the kids. I hope I'm wrong. The next few years were riddled with guilt over my answer. Should I have gone back to an unhappy marriage of abuse in order to be with my babies?

When I drove Caroline "home" that Saturday, Joey's entire family was there to smirk and give me sly looks. They were gloating. They were also giving Caroline a huge fifth birthday party—more for my benefit, I'm sure. I thought about the tiny cake I had bought her, and the couple of friends from the apartment complex who had come over. I had barely been able to buy her a tiny toy for her birthday.

When we arrived, I tried to sound excited for her, and she squealed in excitement, knowing she was about to have some fun. She was grinning from ear to ear and asking me all kinds of questions. "Is this party for me? Is everyone here for me?" She gave me a hug as I pulled her boxes of toys and clothes out of the car. She was clueless that, according to the divorce decree, I wouldn't see her again until Christmas morning.

She ran off to Joey's family, who were applauding her. They were actually applauding Joey's win. I had hoped to see Tony, but he stayed hidden in the crowd. I think there may have been some guilt on his part, and I just wanted him to know that everything was okay. I didn't blame him, not at all. This whole fiasco was my fault. It could have been handled differently. That night I went with my roommate to a bar, drank too much, and had my first of a string of one-night stands.

I did everything I could to stop the pain of losing my babies. If I wasn't out at night, I would toss and turn in my bed until about two or three in the morning, and then I'd go to work. I sat down and drew up a budget, and I discovered that after paying the majority of the bills and child support, I would be short $200 with each paycheck. I didn't know what to do. My boss allowed me to work as much overtime as I could. I started working between sixty and a hundred hours a week in order to have enough gas to go and get the kids every other weekend starting in January. I also had Wednesday night visitations from 6:00 to 8:00.

After a couple of months, I started returning to my senses. I was forced to go through bankruptcy. This brought a little financial relief. Now when I did my budget, I zeroed out instead of having negative numbers after each paycheck. The agony of losing the kids eased just a fraction. But I felt like a hollowed-out piece of a woman. What woman—what *good* mother—loses custody of her children? The shame of not fighting for them never went away.

I became a professional victim. I was tired. I wanted a man to rescue me. I wanted my knight in shining armor to ride up and marry me and help me get custody of my kids. During the next several years, I floated between relationships.

When my lease expired on my apartment, I moved in with a guy I'd only known for a few weeks. His name was Will. His family owned a small, run-down ranch with run-down horses over an hour away from my job. Will managed the ranch. His only income was from the occasional sale of a horse or bales of hay. I knew that relationship was a fiasco when I was rearranging a bedroom and turned around to find a snake on top of the box I had just moved. It was only a chicken snake, but who cared? It was *huge*! I'll never forget being eye-to-eye with that serpent as its tongue flicked in and out of its mouth. I jumped on the bed and screamed and screamed for what seemed like hours. Will finally sauntered in and had the audacity to tell me that I was overreacting. That was all it took. I broke his heart when I left and found another apartment about ten minutes from work.

My "man-picker" was definitely broken. I had an affair with a married man for a year and a half. He was actually seven years older than me, but he was a singer and talented musician who was a natural on the stage. He and his wife were great friends. She was gay, and they were hiding that fact from their son. The fact that she was gay was our justification that our relationship was okay. Of course, that type of relationship never lasts. It doesn't matter why someone is cheating on his spouse. Being the "other woman" is never the relationship that God intended for his daughters. I, of course, ended up wanting more from him than he felt he could give me. When we finally broke up, I actually had to ask him to break up with me because I wasn't strong enough to do it. He accommodated that request and stayed married a few more years!

About six months later, Glen moved in with me. Glen and I met at a C&W club. He was an amazing dancer. He was also ten years younger than I was. I don't know what it is about secular music and lust, but they work together to our detriment. Since he was such a great dancer, and we had let music rule our emotions, it took me a good year to face facts—the first fact being that he had gone through thirteen jobs in twelve months. He was a huge drain on me financially. The second fact was that my kids disliked him *intensely*. The reason I stayed with him? You see, after the first relationship, I had actually made a bargain with the God that I wasn't sure about. I'd said, "God, if you'll just send me someone who loves me, *truly* loves me, I know I'll love him back." Even though I know that God only hears the prayers of the saved, I sometimes wonder if He didn't chuckle at that one and give me exactly what I had asked for, just to prove a point. Glen was passionate about everything in his life: dancing, me, his friendships. He also took that passion to his jobs, feeling that he should be treated with more respect than he received.

Glen lived with me in my apartment for about six months before he decided that we should be living in a house. I passed this notion off as a pie-in-the-sky dream, another one of his notions that always cost me more money. I didn't feel ready to be a homeowner. Truly, from the bottom of my soul, I didn't feel that I deserved a home. After all, I had never really had one. When I was a child, my family had floated around from house to house. I had lived in a mobile home during my marriage. Only people who had their act together, who didn't lose their children in a divorce, could actually own a home. It's amazing the jails that we put ourselves in!

One night, just as I walked in from work, I got a call from a real estate agent telling me that Glen had contacted him and that he would be happy to assist me in buying a home. I was astounded. I was also furious with Glen for putting me in this position. I knew I didn't have the credit, and I was going to be humiliated. If Glen had been home at that moment, I'm not sure what I would have done. I hate secrecy, and I hate lies, and he had gone behind my back and set up that call. There was no way I could afford a house!

But the agent told me that I would be surprised at what I could afford, and he offered to take us house-hunting. He actually followed through on his word and set up an appointment for me with an agency that worked with a bank and got me approved for a home loan with payments I could afford. Wow! Could it actually be possible that I could buy a house? Maybe that would be enough to get my kids back! By this time I had spent three years being the "visiting" parent and about two years of seeing another woman being a stepmother to my babies. I desperately wanted my kids back. Maybe this would be a step!

I started getting excited as the weekend approached. We were going house-hunting. I was approved for a home loan. Wow! I glanced out of the window as I was getting dressed and felt a nudge of fear as our Texas skies started showing signs of imminent storms. I knew these clouds, and yes, there were tornado warnings out that day. But the agent was undeterred. He picked us up, and we went from one run-down house to another.

I could feel my heart sinking. The excitement and anticipation of being a homeowner was waning fast. This was all I could afford? I could feel myself going into a depression. I was also becoming very resentful toward Glen for reminding me exactly where I was in my life. I was nobody. I wasn't even a good enough mother to give her kids a decent home. I sat silently in the backseat as we drove from one miserable house to another.

Then the agent pulled over to take a phone call, and I dejectedly peered out of the window. It had been storming the entire day. I'll never forget looking up at the sky, searching for possible tornado clouds, when suddenly the rain just stopped. That made me nervous. When you live in Tornado Alley, you know that's a warning sign to heed! But there was a momentary burst of sunshine through the clouds. The sun came streaming down and poured out on a nicer home. It was no mansion by any means, but it was better than the ones we had been looking at. It had a *For Sale* sign in the yard, which had been knocked down. When the agent hung up, I pointed the house out to him, and he made a phone call to see if we could get in. He warned me before we went in that they were asking about $15,000 over what I had been approved for. But now I was curious. It was so much better than the other houses we'd been looking at.

As I walked around the house, I knew that even though it wasn't a really nice house, it was a good house. It had a nice backyard and was within sight of the community swimming pool. I sighed inwardly, knowing that I could never afford it. Why had I put myself into a situation that I knew would be a disappointment? But my agent sent the owners an offer, and they accepted! They were in a hurry to sell!

I was ecstatic. It was also not far from where my kids were living. I always wondered if God let that ray of sunshine fall on the house that day, and if He had possibly knocked down the *For Sale* sign so that only I would see it.

After we moved into the house, Glen was still contributing nothing toward the household expenses, which were now substantially higher than the cost of living in an apartment. There were times when I even had to make his truck payment. One night as I sat at my company computer going over the spreadsheet I used to track my expenses, I found myself having to make a decision that I should never have had to make. Did I make Glen's truck payment, or did I see my kids on the weekend? I always budgeted for the groceries I would need when they were with me, and I tried to do at least one fun thing before I took them home—like a dollar movie or bowling.

As I actually found myself having to choose, something in me snapped. I had had enough. Glen's name was not on the house. He had contributed nothing toward the down payment. After he had lived there for six months with free room and board, I finally asked him to leave and not come back. The kids were ecstatic.

About a year later, I fell in love with Ray. He was fourteen years younger than I was. Yes, life was a little better, but my "picker" was still broken. We dated for a year before I came to my senses and walked away from a poisonous relationship. He was a go-getter. He was able to care for himself. But let's just say that his life was very dysfunctional. I happen to know that he's now been happily married for many years and has accepted salvation through our Lord, Jesus. This time, though, I walked away with my head up. (That was a first!) Again, the kids were ecstatic!

There were a few more men scattered throughout these years that I kept from the kids. I was truly, truly lost as I searched for love, acceptance, and security.

A Note from My Blog:
Godly Women Waiting for Godlly Men

Single Moms, Put Your Kids First

June 18, 2011 at 12:33 a.m.

There are a few things I want to accomplish in my life. My number-one passion is to help single moms make better choices than I did. My number-two passion is to help all females make God-based decisions. But God has specifically placed single moms on my heart.

One important lesson I learned—almost too late—was that my children had to come before any man. That should have been a no-brainer. As a mother, I'm sure we all believe that we shouldn't have to be told that. But I have to say that my desire to be with whatever man was in my life made me make stupid choices. I believed I was putting my children first, and if push came to shove, I would have chosen my child over any man; but I still made stupid choices in order to be with someone I believed I loved.

This is important, you single moms out there. This is important for every woman who may ever be a single mother for any reason. When you are *dating* a man, your number-one priority should be the welfare and happiness of your children. When you are engaged, those priorities may shift a little, but your children still come first. If you are blessed to find a man worthy of becoming a part of your family, and you marry, *then* your husband comes first. But until that day comes, if he is a man of God, he will understand and agree with your choices. A man that you are dating should never, ever be placed over your child. If he forces you to choose, I would suggest that you re-evaluate your choice in men.

As I've stressed over and over and over: go with what you know and not with what you feel. Jeremiah 17:9 (NASB) says, "The heart is more deceitful than all else and is desperately sick; Who can understand it?" Our hearts can get us into so much trouble. We listen to the world say, "Follow your heart." What we need to listen to is the Holy Spirit reminding us that Jesus says to follow Him.

53

One more valuable lesson I learned before it was too late was that I was forgiven. Once I accepted the forgiveness of Jesus Christ, I went to my children and asked for their forgiveness. I promised them that they would never see another boyfriend spend the night in our home. I promised them that I would set the example and stand by God's Word and no longer condone sex outside of marriage.

I will admit to slipping from that promise about seven years later for a few weeks, and I crawled back to God with a broken heart filled with repentance after my fall. This time I healed faster and held a new resolve to stick with what I believed God wanted for me, and I was able to live a happy, full life. And when I met my godly man six years later, I was honest about my past and what I believed. He could have rejected such a woman with a past, and I would have understood, but it would not have broken me, because I had accepted God's forgiveness. I do thank God for the man I married and for his leadership and godly counsel, but I could not have appreciated such a man had I not accepted God's forgiveness first.

We are women of God. He *loves* us! So, if you are in the middle of a relationship that is not worthy of a godly woman, pray and make some wise decisions. It may mean breaking your heart, but do the right thing. If you have made mistakes in your past and don't believe that you are worthy of such a man, then it's possible that you haven't accepted the forgiveness that Jesus Christ offers.

Did you know that Jesus prayed for you before you were born? In John 17:20–23, He prayed, "My prayer is not for them alone. I pray also for those who will believe in me through their message, that all of them may be one, Father, just as you are in me and I am in you. May they also be in us so that the world may believe that you have sent me. I have given them the glory that you gave me, that they may be one as we are one: I in them and you in me. May they be brought to complete unity to let the world know that you sent me and have loved them even as you have loved me."

Hold your head high, my sisters. How could anyone doubt a love like the love from the one who died for us. You are loved, my sisters. You are *so* loved! Now, my prayer is that you live like it!

Lesson Learned

"Above all else, guard your heart, for it is the wellspring of life" (Proverbs 4:23 NASB).

What is a wellspring? Webster's online dictionary says it's "something or someone that provides a large amount of something: a good source *of* something."

Our heart provides a large amount of love, and God's Word says that it provides a large amount of life. We are to guard that source! We must guard against temptations of all kinds, like sex and pornography. (Yes, women can become addicts too.)

Jesus was very clear. If you even look at someone with lust, you've committed adultery. This wasn't only spoken to married men. It was said to the crowd at the Sermon on the Mount, and there were women there.

My problem was that I was looking for a man to make everything better, to help me get custody of my children. I sought this help by sleeping with them. I knew something wasn't right. I knew I felt cheap and used. My whole lifestyle involved living outside of God's will. And my soul was being shredded.

CHAPTER 4

Adjusting the Rearview Mirror and Looking Ahead: Finding a New Path

Warning:
Enter through the narrow gate. For wide is the gate
and broad is the road that leads to destruction, and
many enter through it. But small is the gate and narrow
the road that leads to life, and only a few find it.
— Matthew 7:13

After I broke up with Ray, I had a new resolve: to be a better mother to my kids. Money was still tight, but I was doing much better financially. But something was still missing in my life. I had the money to pay my bills, and I saw my kids frequently. What was missing?

Part of my job involved working with our Denver office. My main contact there was the administrative assistant, Candace (or Candy, as we called her). She was an amazing woman (and I'm sure she still is). She loved the Lord, loved her husband, sewed clothes for her kids, kept a beautiful home, and worked hard at her job. She was one of "those" women who just seemed to do it all and do it well. And she could sing. She had one of those voices that made people stop and stare because it was so amazing.

One of the great aspects of my job was the opportunity to work closely with Candy. We had some great personal conversations over the phone during our lunch hours. On one of those occasions, sometime in 1992 just a year after I'd left Joey, I got a call from Candy, and her voice was filled with excitement.

"Honey! Honey! Oh my goodness! This weekend I went to an amazing service at my church!"

I immediately felt myself shutting down. I admired Candy's faith, but I could feel that old wall of resistance rise up when she started talking about it. I really didn't want to hear any "God talk," but I wanted to hear what had happened that was so exciting to her, so I kept the conversation going.

"Really?" I tried to muffle the boredom as best I could.

"Yes!" she responded. "God told us that at some time in everybody's life He will call our name."

"Wait, wait," I interrupted her. "What do you mean? Like 'whooo, ghost-type' stuff?"

I could almost hear her grin over the phone. "No," she replied in mock exasperation, "but have you ever been alone in your house or maybe walking down the street when you think you hear your name being called?"

"Yes," I answered, finding myself becoming more and more intrigued, albeit grudgingly.

"Well, what do you do?"

I thought about it and finally said, "I either tell myself I'm hearing things, or I turn to see if someone is there."

"Exactly!" she said triumphantly.

I was confused to say the least. "And?" I prompted her.

"Well, according to my pastor, our response should be, 'I am here, Lord. How may I serve You?'"

I almost wanted to hang up on her. Honestly, I did. I loved her, and I admired her faith in something that I believed *could* be legitimate, but … "Wow, that's interesting," I replied and mentally shrugged my shoulders.

"But that's not the exciting part!" she exclaimed. "Last night I fell asleep, and then I woke up because I heard my name being called!"

Mentally I slapped my forehead and rolled my eyes. "So, what are you supposed to do to serve the Lord?" I asked (but only because I knew she wanted me to ask).

"Sing! I'm supposed to sing for the Lord. I don't know if it's by being in a choir or pursuing a singing career, but I'm supposed to sing for Him!"

I could believe that. Her voice was wonderful. However, I filed this information away and never thought of it again. I think Candy was a little disappointed that I wasn't more receptive, but she knew better than to push me. Little did either of us know that a seed had been sown into my life in that very moment.

Shortly after that conversation, Candy moved to Tennessee. I had no way of contacting her, and I've thought about her often over the years. It's so hard now to realize how easily a friendship can slip away without cell phones or e-mail or Facebook. Even today, if you don't have a current, past, or maiden name, you're still stuck. I truly still miss her!

As the years flew along, I started opening up my mind to the idea that maybe I was missing something on the spiritual side. But my marriage wasn't annulled, as far as I knew, and I didn't know what kind of church to go to. I had heard phrases like "a Bible-believing church," but what did that mean? I mean, really, didn't everybody pretty much interpret the Bible as they saw fit? I was so confused that I even let a friend talk me into trying Scientology. I went to a couple of meetings in 1996, but as many of you know, it's a money-making machine, and each visit was more expensive than the last. I had to stop at the third visit. If finding myself was going to be expensive, forget it! (Maybe it was a blessing that I was broke. Could it be that God used my poverty to protect me from myself? Yes, I do believe this.)

In September of 1997, I was doing a little bit of online dating, mainly out of pure boredom. I wasn't going out much. I was still filled with guilt over the way I'd handled my divorce. I often overcompensated with my kids by giving them too much and never going out. If I wanted friendship, my friends were a phone call away. I was working hard and mothering hard. If I had the kids, then I had the kids. I was relearning how to be the kind of mother they needed me to be while having as little contact with their dad as I could.

At one point during the online dating, a pastor from Vermont actually contacted me. Wow! A pastor! When he asked me for my phone number, I was thrilled. Our conversations lasted for hours. I never asked how a pastor from a small, rural church in Vermont could afford these phone calls. Remember, this was before cell phones were common. We talked and flirted and enjoyed some great conversations. I know I should have cut him off when I found out that I was eight years older than he was. But the more I said that there was no way it could work, the more he insisted that it could. When I mentioned the age difference, he didn't care. When I mentioned the physical distance, he said he'd love to move to the south. He was telling me that he loved me after our third or fourth time talking. I remember asking him what God thought about sex outside of marriage.

His answer was, "I think God made us all sexual creatures, and He sees nothing wrong with it." Hey! Maybe my past few years had not been as sinful as I'd thought! I was intrigued. Guilt-free sex! Who would've known? Was I getting an answer?

Finally, after a month of conversations through instant messaging and over the phone, Sean flew me to Vermont. I'll never forget getting off the plane and looking up and seeing him. He was a good-looking man. I'll also never forget seeing the frozen look of disappointment on his face. Immediately my heart fell.

I was actively doing aerobics and trying to keep my body in shape, but a woman knows when a man is disappointed in what he is seeing. However, on our two-hour drive to his home, he reached over and held my hand, and I started feeling hopeful again. After that first night together, I could tell that he was no longer interested in pursuing a relationship. He was just like every other man I had dealt with from my past of one-night stands (though those days had been put behind me).

During the remainder of my stay, he was always polite. We still had sex, of course, and he took me out to dinner. He was thoughtful and courteous, even though he did have a sermon to work on. I tried my best to be quiet and stay out of his way. I prowled around his house and grabbed some books.

In Sean's study, his desk sat under this amazing picture of Jesus. This painting was unique. It was unlike any picture of Jesus that I had ever seen before. In this painting, Jesus wasn't scowling or serious or ethereal. This picture was so different! It was … amazing! Jesus was grinning! It was a secretive, mischievous grin that made me see a human side to this "ghost god" that I had been raised to know. But it made sense that Jesus would've smiled about some things, right? He didn't just come here as a holier-than-thou being who floated across the earth. He was here as God, and He was here as man.

Over the next few days, I cuddled up on an overstuffed chair across the room from Sean's desk and that painting. One of the books had a title that intrigued me. It was *The Shroud* by Ian Wilson. Books on religion were pretty much all there was to read in the home of a pastor, and I did have a lot of questions, so I grudgingly started to read it. It wasn't long before I was wanting to cross-reference what the author was saying with what was in the Bible.

I had never desired to pick up the Bible before. I was quickly pulled into the book, into the life and death of Jesus, and was taking a step into a whole new way of thinking. I would read a bit and then sit and stare at the picture of Jesus above Sean's desk. As I read this book, which broke down each type of torture that His body was put through, my heart began to stir. I would read and then bring my gaze up to that picture. I began to know a grieving unlike anything I had ever experienced. I would gaze at those laughing, human eyes and then read what had actually happened to his very human body, and my eyes would tear up. Was this what I was looking for? Was this the missing piece in my life? What Satan had meant for evil on this trip,

God was definitely using for good. This was the start of something new for me. It made me start thinking and asking questions. But yes, my man-picker was still broken.

When I got home, I started listening to some sermons on the radio and actually listened to the words of some Christian hymns. Though my heart was once again broken and my soul had another hole, it was opening to something way bigger than myself. My life felt like it was finally going in a good direction. I loved my job. Legally, my daughter would be coming to live with me soon. I was just waiting for the judge's signature, which could be months in coming. There was excitement in the air.

My job was opening new doors for me. I was taking on more responsibilities that I loved. I was learning new software, and I made the decision that I should learn how to develop websites. If you know anything about HTML or website design software, you know that learning this on your own can be really difficult, to say the least. But it was a challenge, and I loved it! As I progressed with my thirst for Jesus and my thirst for web design, I played around with trying to develop a website. I was actually blogging before there was a word *blog*. I truly wish I had kept all of the old files, because they showed my walk going from a seeker to accepting Christ.

Once I learned how to publish a website, I became excited. Once I learned how graphics worked, I became more excited. The night I figured out how all of that worked together was really exciting! That night was October 9, 1998. Why would I remember that date, you ask? It was the night that changed my life.

On this night, I went to bed very excited. For some reason, I prayed that night. I specifically said, "Lord, please hit me over the head and make me understand what I need to understand." I lay there for a while, contemplating the direction my life was going. I finally fell into a very deep, welcome sleep.

Several hours later, this voice yelled, "*Honey!*"

I sat straight up in bed and shouted, "What?"

It felt as though the room had been filled with that voice, but at the same time, it was behind me. Was it outside? My body shook with the vibration I had just experienced. My heart was beating so fast. I just *knew* my house was on fire. I was so scared.

This part of the story would actually make a great comedic skit as I look back on it. I had an old water bed with a full-motion mattress. I was kicking off the covers and trying to vault myself over the side of the bed in a full-blown panic. The bed was heaving and moving and not letting me get out. I hated that bed at that moment! And the whole time my mind was racing, thinking, "I don't smell smoke. If someone's in my backyard, why isn't Taz (my dog) barking?"

About that time, I pulled the curtains back, half afraid that someone's face would be staring back at me, and there was Taz, sitting in the most beautiful pool of moonlight. It was so surreal after the loudness and explosion of emotion I had just felt. Just as my senses were coming into focus on the serenity of the scene, Taz started *howling*! Loudly! Eerily!

That did it. I jumped back into bed, pulled the covers over my head, and shook. I seriously sat there on my rocking water bed with the covers pulled over my head, trying to figure out what in the world had just happened.

Then Candy's words came back to me. Slowly, the words she had told me years ago started to come back to me. "What do you do when you hear your name called?"

I swallowed, and feeling kind of foolish, I said, "I'm here, Lord. How may I serve You?" It was worth a try. After all, hadn't I prayed and asked Him to hit me over the head?

Well, I sat and waited in scared anticipation. My body was quaking, shaking, and shivering with emotion. I was crying and praying. Then I found myself repenting for the next four hours. I asked Jesus into my life with a full heart. I released all of the years of abuse and neglect, and all of the heartbreaks. I was a new person.

And still I waited and waited for an answer to my question: "How may I serve You?" But there was nothing. There were no great revelations, no more voices. But I knew I had just experienced something extraordinary.

So, as my room started growing lighter with the new morning, I continued to pray. "Lord, I *think* that was You last night. At least I'm pretty sure, but I need some help here. Can you give me a sign that it was You and leave me no room for doubt? I want to serve You, and I need Your guidance." I had heard rumors that Satan could disguise himself, and I was taking no chances! I mean, if I was going to believe in a heavenly Father who was good, that meant there was also evil, right?

On my way to work that morning, I was elated, tired but elated. I was so happy; I couldn't explain it. As I was driving and asking over and over, "How may I serve You?," a slow inpouring of knowledge came to me—the knowledge that I was supposed to write something … something. I couldn't put my finger on it. I was talking to one of my coworkers about it when the phone rang.

This voice came over the phone: "Honey? This is Candace! I had this feeling I was supposed to call you." Several years had gone by since we had last talked, and it was a little longer than that since she'd told me about God's calling her to sing. I was late for a meeting, but I needed to talk to her.

I started crying. "Candy? I can't believe it! I was just talking about you! The voice, Candy! I heard it last night."

Her voice was very warm and reassuring, reaching out to me. "Congratulations, sweetie. What are you supposed to do to serve the Lord?"

A Note from My Blog:
Godly Women Waiting for Godlly Men

Comparing Our Pain

January 1, 2012 at 6:23 p.m.

I had a temporary crown fall off my tooth today. Immediately I started preparing myself mentally for the pain I knew would be coming. Would it throb? Would it be sharp? How fast could I get to the store to buy some toothache medicine? How soon would the dentist be able to see me tomorrow?

As I waited, a thought came to me. How did Jesus feel, knowing exactly the treatment His body would suffer? Did you see the movie, *The Passion of the Christ*? Can you imagine what it would be like *knowing* that you would be facing that pain? Can you imagine knowing that your suffering *had* to happen, not only in fulfillment of the Scriptures but for our very salvation? He took on that pain for everyone, knowing the agony ahead of time.

So how can anyone seriously worry about whether or not we can go months or years without sex or having a man touch us in a loving way? How can I sit here with a tooth that may or may not start to hurt and worry about it? Doesn't it seem so trivial? He grew up knowing how His earthly body would die and in what manner it would be terminated. All He asks of us is our everything, which is the most freeing way of living. Can you do it? Can you sit and contemplate what He went through for your eternal life? It's something to think about.

Lesson Learned

"And everyone who calls on the name of the Lord will be saved" (Acts 2:21).

Candace immediately knew what I was talking about when I said, "The voice!" My reply to her question was, "Write. Somehow I'm supposed to write."

Her reply was, "It'll come to you."

I had asked God to show me that I had been dealing with Him through that night. I had asked Him because I needed to make sure that I had heard from *Him*. Could God have responded to me any more clearly? It had been years since Candace and I had talked! And what better scenario could He have set up for me, except to get a call from the original "seed dropper" all those years ago. And she said she felt she was being led to call me—on the morning after such a miraculous night. Wow!

My nose-to-the-carpet night was almost like a wedding night. When I asked Jesus to come into my heart, to take my pain and make it into something good, He became my husband! From that moment on, I walked under His protection in His love and started running my problems through His Word. What a great setup for what was to come!

CHAPTER 5

Eyes on the Road: Which Road? Finding a New Life as a Christian

Warning:
The fear of the LORD is the beginning of wisdom,
And the knowledge of the Holy One is understanding.
—Proverbs 9:10

One weekend a few weeks before Caroline came to live with me, I found myself alone and wondering what to do with myself. Caroline was still with her dad, but it was only a matter of days or weeks before she'd be with me. She had just turned twelve years old. Even with the knowledge of her coming, I went into a full-blown pity party. I started crying, actually sobbing from heartbreak and loneliness. Every woman who has ever been single knows that, no matter how strong you are, there are moments when you cave and allow yourself to feel the loneliness. You allow it to wash over you. Then you shake it off and get on with your life.

Once I pulled myself out of the muck and mire of my self-indulgence in loneliness, I started praying: "Lord, I just want to laugh. I don't really care that much about dating or meeting someone. I just want to laugh! Please?" He reminded me of this prayer about a year later.

It was my daughter who suggested that we try to find a church. Actually, she almost begged me to find a church. I'm still not sure what was driving her to push me to find a place for us. Maybe she felt she was missing something. However, I was conflicted.

First of all, Caroline had been raised Catholic, but according to the teachings I had learned, I was no longer welcome in the Catholic church. As a matter of fact, from what I had been told—*implied* from the pulpit and frankly *spoken* by fellow Catholics—I was going to hell!

But honestly, I thought that since I had found the Lord and now felt His love, the Catholics couldn't be right about me. I knew Jesus as my Lord and Savior, and I had repented and turned away from my former ways. So what should I do? I didn't *feel* like I was going to hell, but ... I was also conflicted by the fact that I was working so many hours that I felt I really needed Sundays to sleep in. But for my daughter's sake, I knew I needed to find out if I would actually be welcomed into a church as a divorced woman and single mother.

One Friday I picked up Caroline and Tony from their dad's house, and she told me that we had been invited to church by one of her friends. Tony wanted no part of it. Caroline and I attended for about a month, but then we fell back into the habit of sleeping late on Sundays. It was easy to do, as I had felt pushed out of this particular church. Most of the congregation was married, and there just wasn't a sense of being welcome. While there was truth in what I felt, I was also looking for excuses to sleep! Caroline wasn't too excited about it, either. I wanted to know more about this awesome God, and who Jesus Christ really was, but I wasn't learning. Still, God had other plans for me.

During this time, learning how to do web design had become a full-blown hobby of mine. I had even started a prayer page, sharing the prayers of strangers, and updating as God answered. One day a woman contacted me and asked for prayer because she was about to lose her children through divorce. They were very young. Her daughter was just a baby, not even walking yet, and her son was only a toddler. My heart bled for her. I wanted so badly to help her. Here I was, a new Christian still seeking a church home, not knowing what direction to take with my life—and I wanted to help someone.

I asked if she could meet me for lunch one day. She was so excited to accept the offer, and we became instant friends. Her story broke my heart over and over again. Her name was Alaina. What was so ironic about our meeting was the fact that although she had the deep faith of a more mature Christian and was quite a bit younger than me, I had the experience of a more mature woman who knew what she was facing in her custody fight. We needed each other. The difference in our Christian maturity was confirmed when she just assumed that I was going to pray out loud over our lunch. I was mortified and hurriedly told her that she could do it. God's plan was just beginning to unfold itself to me.

As we ate our lunch and I listened to her story, I knew that she was definitely going to lose her children. Her ex-husband had the money, and she was broke. The best I could do was give her practical advice on how the court system worked (or didn't) and what my experiences were. She listened and asked a lot of questions, and before I knew it, my lunch hour was over.

Before we parted, she said, "Hey, what church do you attend?" I was embarrassed to tell her that I wasn't attending one. In my head I was thinking, *How dare I have a prayer page when I'm not even going to a church?*

"Do you want to come with me to my church on Sunday?" she asked.

I was hesitant, I have to admit. I wanted a church where my daughter would feel comfortable going, one that was biblically sound. That was my number-one priority. Remember, I was still a baby Christian. I didn't know *what* my priorities were supposed to be!

"Where do you go to church?" I reluctantly asked. She named a well-known mega church. I was even more conflicted. It was a *huge* church. Just hearing the name intimidated me.

"Um, let me think about it. I know that's a huge church. I don't think I'm ready for that."

She accepted my answer but made the offer several times over the next few months. I kept finding excuses not to go.

As the next few months flew by, Alaina and I became good friends. She accepted my reluctance to attend her church with grace. She didn't push me away or give up on me. As my forty-first birthday rolled around, I asked her if she'd like to come to my house to celebrate it with me. What made that night even better was that she was sitting at my table when my front door burst open and in walked Caroline with a box full of clothes. Then, in walked my son carrying more boxes.

"What's going on?" I asked, not daring to believe that my prayers had been answered.

"Caroline's moving in tonight," my son calmly stated.

I was in shock. I had been patiently waiting for the judge to sign the papers. As it turned out, the papers had been lost in the system, but it took us weeks to realize it. I was in constant contact with my attorney, especially since I was getting daily phone calls from a crying daughter begging me to come and get her.

I had begged her not to lose faith in me and to keep praying for the paperwork to work its way through the court system. She didn't understand. She was only eleven. And now, here she was, with no warning or phone call from her father. What a birthday!

But one of the hardest parts of that night was watching my son walk out the door without his sister. I'll never forget the slumped shoulders and the half-hearted wave he gave as he left. I had never wanted them separated. Never.

Now that Caroline was living with me, she began to push harder to find a church. I finally allowed Alaina to talk me into going to her church. I waited for a weekend where Caroline was at her dad's house. I wasn't going to subject her to anything until I had checked it out first.

That Sunday I attended a Bible study for singles. I loved the lesson. I loved the laughter. And I really loved the social activities on their calendar. But the real test was going to be at the worship service. Would I find that extra "something" in a mega church? The answer was a resounding yes. I had to ask myself why it was a mega church.

Could it possibly be that God's hand was on the pastor, the staff, and the congregation? Absolutely.

I was blissfully surprised at my response to this pastor. He blew me away. He had a sense of humor, and he answered my questions straight from the Bible. The Word came alive for me. I was so excited. I knew I had found a church home. I couldn't wait for Caroline to join me the next week.

As the following week came to a close, I knew Caroline was excited to see this church I had been talking about. As we walked into the huge building together and found her Bible study, I could see her eyes dancing as she looked around the room full of kids her age. There were even a few kids there that she knew. Everything in me knew that this was good.

After my Bible study I found my way back to her classroom. She was brimming with good things to say. We left her class to attend our first worship service together. We both listened intently to everything the pastor had to say. As we were leaving to join my class for lunch, she said, "Mom, I understood everything he was saying. Can we keep coming here?" I can't explain how happy this mother's heart was. A few weeks later, on Mother's Day, my daughter and I came forward and joined the church. I wish I could say that my son joined with us, but by this time he was calling himself an atheist.

After walking the seemingly endless aisle to shake the pastor's hand, we sat and talked to someone from the church. When the young lady asked me if I believed I was saved, I answered yes. She asked me how I knew, and I answered, "Because I believe that Jesus died on the cross for my sins. I believe he died and rose again and is seated at the right hand of the Father." Funny, that was when I realized what the Apostle's Creed truly meant—after all those years of being a Catholic! Caroline couldn't give the same answer. And this was where I made a critical error.

I knew I needed to be baptized. But instead of going ahead and doing it, I waited for Caroline to reach a point where she could get baptized. One evening a lady from the church called and asked if I'd like to schedule my baptism, and I explained to her why I was waiting. Her response shook me to the core. She said, "Dear, I'd like you to think about this: the decision to get baptized is strictly between you and God, just as your daughter's decision is strictly between *her* and God. Neither decision should be put on hold for the other."

I was such a baby Christian, and I wanted to be obedient. I had jumped into my love of Christ with both feet, and I wanted the world to know it. And I wanted my daughter (and my son) to know it. As I've said, you know truth when you hear it. I told the lady that I would call her back. I found Caroline in her room and told her that I was going to get baptized in a couple of weeks during the Sunday evening service. She was okay with that.

About a week before I was to get baptized, Caroline told me that she was ready to be baptized also. I made sure that a pastor spoke with her, and we both eagerly looked forward to that Sunday!

I told Caroline to make sure she invited her dad, Tony, and their stepmom to come and watch, but the entire family from her father's side did nothing but create chaos and turmoil in what should have been an awesome milestone in her life. As far as they were concerned, we were both going to hell for going outside of the Catholic faith. Her dad steadfastly refused to come, and so did her brother. We were both sad about that but more resolved than ever do this.

My new friends from the Bible study were going to come that evening, including Alaina, and we all planned to go to dinner afterward. But once again, God's hand was about to move.

That afternoon I got a phone call from my boss. "Honey, we need you back at work as quickly as possible. We have a virus, and we need to shut it down now."

I was flabbergasted. E-mail and the Internet were both relatively new at the time. We were a fast-rising company that didn't realize the importance of virus protection—yet. I quickly informed him that I was getting baptized in a few hours and that my friends were taking me and my daughter out to dinner.

His response was, "You're going to have to skip the dinner. As soon as the service is over, you need to come to work. I'm sorry, but we need you."

I was dismayed that I'd miss the dinner, but I knew that my boss needed someone there with access to all of their systems. That someone was me and everyone on my team. However, the rest of my team had lives (at least that was my way of reasoning back then). They were all married. I felt that since I was the team lead and they had "real" families that it was my duty to pull all of the weight. (Yes, I know now that I was wrong.)

That night as I was baptized, the joy I felt was immeasurable. And the sound of the applause that resounded through the church as my baby girl came into the water after me was surreal. I was a new creature in Christ, and while I would have given my life for my son to see this, I wasn't going to spend one second on regret.

I made arrangements for Caroline to spend the night with a friend and go to school the next day. They all went to dinner, and I went to work. I worked through the night, sleeping under my desk between phone calls. We were an international company, and my number was the number that everyone was supposed to call for help during this crisis. I worked through the next day and the next night. I went home for a change of clothes on Tuesday and a quick nap, going back to work and staying until Thursday morning, all the while juggling where Caroline would be staying and trying to make sure she was taken care of. On Wednesday the company brought in a team of contractors that I was to train on handling the virus. It was a relief to get more help. Finally, on Thursday morning I dragged myself home for a shower and a nap. I was utterly exhausted, and I missed my kids!

After I'd slept for a couple of hours, my phone rang. I groggily answered, "Hello?" I was barely coherent, I'm sure. My boss's voice came over the line. There was a slight edge to his voice that I couldn't place, but I figured that he was just worried and exhausted, even though he hadn't put in nearly the hours that I had.

"Honey, we need you back up here."

"Why?" I asked. "I really need to get some sleep." I felt like I had sandpaper in my eyes.

"We just do. Come back now." And he hung up.

I sat there in utter amazement, staring at the phone in my hand.

"What in the world?" I muttered.

I was pretty angry and very tired. I got dressed and slowly drove in to work. There I was met with a line of contractors outside my door.

"What's going on?" I asked. I was bewildered. Why were they not working?

"Your team has been laid off," one of them explained.

I smiled. I was sure they were mistaken. I had become a Christian! I had faith! And outside of that, the company was doing okay. A few weeks earlier I had received a very prestigious award that had come with a very nice bonus. Only five people worldwide had received that award! No, these guys were mistaken.

"Why would you say that?" I asked. I waited for the answer, just knowing that I would be able to knock holes in their reasoning.

"Their accounts are locked, and the VP of IT is talking to them one by one in his office, and they're not returning to their offices.

"I'll take care of that," I answered, and I went to enable their accounts.

But lo and behold, my account had been deactivated! Reality began to sink in. I sighed very deeply. I loved my job. I loved this company. I had been there almost nine years. I looked out the window of the office I had strived so hard to get. I exhaled and felt my whole body deflate.

Then a second flood of reality hit. I had a daughter to support! What was I going to do? I was so tired. For the past eight years, my average work week had been around sixty hours, and many weeks were over one hundred hours, but I loved what I did. As I looked out the window, I saw people leaving. I looked down and knew that I was about to go—kicking and screaming—into a new life.

I saw some packing boxes sitting in the hallway, and I began to pack. By the time my boss came to my office and escorted me to the

VP's office, I was completely packed. I listened to the termination speech, accepted my severance check, and walked out of the building with a security escort. I begged to walk down the stairs instead of using the public elevators, and my boss accommodated my request. It would have killed me to say good-bye to my friends.

I was on first-name basis with most of the security staff. Leaving there was one of the hardest things I had gone through since losing my kids. I have to admit, everyone knew that this past week had been brutal, and now it felt like I was being kicked in the teeth.

But I got in my car, put the top down on my little four-cylinder, used Mustang, and started driving. I didn't have a cell phone at that time, so I stopped at a pay phone and called Alaina. She worked nights, and I hated to wake her up, but I needed a friend. As I heard her voice on the line, I started bawling.

"Hey! It's going to be all right," Alaina said. "Did you get a severance check?" She was trying to distract me from my misery.

"Yes." I sniffed. "I got six months' pay plus three weeks of vacation." I still don't know how she understood what I was saying because I was crying so hard.

She started laughing. "Did you just hear what you said?"

I thought about it and took a second look at the check. Wow! I had never seen that much money all at once! I wish I had immediately turned to God instead of a friend. I wish I had immediately felt a peace in the knowledge that God wasn't surprised. But all of that is part of the Christian growth process, I was finding out.

I know now that when God moves in your life, He doesn't necessarily move a little piece here and there. It's more like your life is a jigsaw puzzle sometimes. And this time he took the whole box of my predictable life and dumped it out. However, after much prayer and encouragement from my friends, my panic settled down a little, and thus began my first step in learning to trust God, wherever He would be taking me.

The funny part was that nobody was surprised. I thought, *I'm a Christian! I'm making good decisions, and now I'm out of a job! What?*

But the more mature Christians in my life were not surprised at all. And now, to be honest, I'm the same way. If I counsel new Christians and become involved in their lives, it doesn't surprise me at all when God starts moving the jigsaw pieces of their lives around.

When I discovered Christ, I dove into love with Him. The Bible says in Revelation 3:15–16, "I know your deeds that you are neither cold nor hot; I wish that you were cold or hot. So because you are lukewarm, and neither hot nor cold, I will spit you out of My mouth."

As my questions about God, heaven, Jesus, and salvation were answered, I only had more questions. I was insatiable. The awesome part was that I was able to apologize to my kids for the men that they had seen in my life, and I promised them that they would never have to worry about anyone being in our home again. I told them that the Bible says that sex outside of marriage is a sin. Period. I was a new creature in Christ, and I wasn't going to do that. I wanted them to trust me and to know that my yes was yes and my no was no. I was determined that they could come to trust me at the deepest level that a child can trust a parent—just as I was coming to trust my heavenly Father.

My job became looking for a job. I volunteered more and more at church and was part of the new leadership that would be moved to our new campus, which was closer to my home. It was an exciting time. Yet there was a niggling worry that I wouldn't be able to find a job. My old job had been one that I had created for myself. I had outlined a need that the company had and had sold my boss and his boss on how I could get it done. I wasn't sure my skills could be used in another company.

After being laid off for about a month, I was at the church one evening and was standing in the gym watching people jog around the jogging path. I voiced my concern about finding a job and man whose name I've now forgotten said some words that truly impacted me.

"Did you get a severance package?" he asked.

I told him that I did.

And he said, "Can you imagine any other time in your life when you will have over six months of paychecks put away, time off of work where you can sleep and catch up on things you've been putting off? God promises you that He'll take care of you. Why not show Him that you have faith and take your daughter on a mini-vacation? For a weekend or so?"

I was astounded. Should I do that? It sounded like I wasn't taking care of my responsibilities if I did that. It was a real struggle for me. But I went home and prayed about it, and the answer was yes. Spend some time with your kids. Go somewhere, but don't be extravagant. Caroline and I pulled out a map of the United States, and she covered her eyes and pointed to the map. Where did her finger land? Atlanta, Georgia. I said, "Um, do you want to try again? Of all the places that you could have picked … Atlanta?" Living in Texas, it's just a little more exciting to get out of the South every once in a while.

Still shaking my head, I called my son and asked him if he wanted to go. I expected him to be excited, but he told me no. I was so disappointed. I almost decided not to go because I felt so guilty planning this trip without him, but I decided to go ahead. He was sixteen and could make that decision if he wanted to. So we found a cheap hotel and cheap airfare, and we flew to Atlanta.

We did a lot of driving around. We visited an old plantation that had a civil war reenactment. We went to Stone Mountain too. It was a really good weekend. I came home refreshed and ready to get back to my job search. And wouldn't you know it? A couple of days later I got a call to start work at a well-known oil services company. I would be making more money but driving a lot farther. I would not have to work one-hundred-hour weeks, and I would be available for my daughter once I got home from work. Is our Abba, our Father, good or what? Only He could have arranged that! Within six weeks I had joined a church, started serving and growing in the Lord, lost my job, and landed on my own two feet, all while being held the whole time in His hands. In all of the turmoil that my life had known, never had something just worked itself out. It was as if someone had a plan.

A Note from My Blog:
Godly Women Waiting for Godlly Men

Crying in the Attic
May 19, 2010 at 10:11 a.m.
I have a couple of "crying in the attic" stories, but after praying, I think this is the one God wanted me to share.
I owned my home. It was storming outside, and I was in my bedroom getting ready for Sunday night Bible study. I just happened to look up, and there was a brown water mark on the ceiling. My heart fell as I realized that there was no water pipe that went over that ceiling. With dread, I pulled down the attic ladder and started climbing. Immediately I heard the water. I turned my eyes reluctantly to the source of the sound, and there was a golf-ball-size hole in the plywood beneath the shingles. Water was just pouring in.
I started crying as I went to find a bucket. I was broke, but I couldn't have this hole in my roof! I was so scared ... and mad! I brought the bucket up and fixed some boards to hold it. And then I just lost it. I started screaming at God. "You *promised* to take care of me! I don't have a husband. I don't have anyone to turn to. Your Word *promises* that You will take care of me! How could you let this happen?" I was sobbing. If anyone was outside, they were probably wondering which was louder, my wailing or the storm!
I sat up there for about ten minutes, crying and feeling sorry for myself and then trying to remember the phone number of a person I had served with in the youth ministry. His name was Lester. I climbed down from the attic, and the storm started letting up, which was a relief. I started looking for Lester's number. I searched my e-mails. I searched my cell phone. It had been a couple of years since I'd talked to him. Oh, well. I decided I might as well go to Bible study.

I was so disheartened. I walked into Bible study, and guess who was there? Yep. It was Lester! We talked, and he came out to my house the next day. I was prepared to pay him in installments. He had to replace the whole board and all of the shingles that covered it. And he wouldn't accept a penny from me. As I wholeheartedly thanked him, he said, "Thank God, not me. I just did what He told me to do." Let it be known that I had never seen Lester in that Bible study before or since!

Of course I had some apologizing to do. I know now that this was a faith-building exercise—one of many. As the years went on and these "things" happened, I gradually learned to fully trust that I would be taken care of. God promises this to us in Matthew 6:25–34.

Therefore I say unto you, be not anxious for your life, what ye shall eat, or what ye shall drink; nor yet for your body, what ye shall put on. Is not the life more than the food, and the body than the raiment? Behold the birds of the heaven, that they sow not, neither do they reap, nor gather into barns; and your heavenly Father feedeth them. Are not ye of much more value then they? And which of you by being anxious can add one cubit unto the measure of his life? And why are ye anxious concerning raiment? Consider the lilies of the field, how they grow; they toil not, neither do they spin: yet I say unto you, that even Solomon in all his glory was not arrayed like one of these. But if God doth so clothe the grass of the field, which to-day is, and to-morrow is cast into the oven, shall he not much more clothe you, O ye of little faith? Be not therefore anxious, saying, What shall we eat? or, What shall we drink? or, Wherewithal shall we be clothed? For after all these things do the Gentiles seek; for your heavenly Father knoweth that ye have need of all these things. But seek ye first his kingdom, and his righteousness; and all these things shall be added unto you. Be not therefore anxious for the morrow: for the morrow will be anxious for itself. Sufficient unto the day is the evil thereof. (Matthew 6:25–34)

Lesson Learned

As a single mom, I've held on to the Scripture verses above like no other. I love this passage so much. I have leaned on it many times, sometimes wondering where my next meal would come from or how I would feed my kids when I had them for the weekend. But He was and is and always will be faithful. He promised. Read that verse again and hold on to it!

CHAPTER 6

Eyes on the Road:
To Date or Not to Date?

Warning:
[It is] better to trust in the LORD than to put confidence in man.
— Psalm 118:8

As a new Christian during this time, I found what appeared to be three types of men. I detest categorizing, but as a woman I find myself doing this. I loosely used these three classifications:

- *Worldly* - These men were so far out in the world that discernment wasn't even necessary. They were usually agnostic or atheistic and were living their lives accordingly.
- *Wolves in sheep's clothing* - These men knew the Bible well. Their words said one thing, but their actions said another. I always needed and relied on God's discernment in these instances.
- *God-fearing men* - These were men who not only knew the Bible but strove to be Christ-like.

I wanted a God-fearing man. I wanted one badly. But was I ready? It appeared that men had totally stopped looking in my direction—and that those who did were nowhere near the type of godly man

I longed for. Why had men stopped looking at me with any type of interest at all? This was a new experience for me. In the secular world, men read the desperation in my eyes and took advantage of it. Now I was being totally ignored. I also found out that it was very easy to transfer my old habit of admiring the "star" on the stage in a club to admiring the "star" in front of the Bible study class—or just about any man who could recite from the Bible. But God was working in this area of my life. If I found myself attracted to a man, I learned to stand back and study him. I didn't flirt at all.

It was easy to admire men who knew Christ or at least who appeared to know Him. But down deep I knew that I wasn't ready for a godly relationship. I would have fallen head over heels and probably would have tried to entice him to bed in order to get the commitment. I still wasn't healed, but I was learning to recognize that fact. I truly believe that God placed a hedge of protection around my newly found innocence. He protected me as long as I protected my heart.

The first step I took toward finding out how to live my newfound Christian singleness was to start reading. My first book was *Ten Commandments of Dating* by Ben Young. This was *it*! Though written for a much younger audience, God's expectations still applied to me. I devoured that book and highly recommend it to a single person of any age who wants to know how God expects us to act.

The author had me at chapter 1: "Thou Shalt Get a Life." He talked about heartbreak and the desperation of a needy person. I was hooked. I finally had a direction that I understood. I wanted a life! I wanted to be busy and be happy with "just" being a mother and a hardworking bread-earner.

I started devouring every book on being a single Christian that I could find. I was hungry, and I was thirsty!

After a couple of years of being in the church, reading, trying to be the best person I could be, and trying to be a light in the darkness, I read a book that truly impacted me. The impact must have been so great that I loaned it out to a friend, because I cannot find it, and I've forgotten the name and who the author was. Since I must have read it over fifteen years ago, I beg forgiveness for forgetting! But in that book there was a chapter directed specifically to single mothersespecially single mothers with teen-aged daughters. I read and reread that chapter, because I did *not* like what it said.

The author was telling me not to date until my daughter was out of the house! I was not prepared for that. I think I still had a remnant of hope that I'd meet Mr. Right, and he'd be such a great man that my son would move in with me and accept Christ. And my daughter would have a good model of what a godly man looked like, and we'd all live happily ever after. This author was asking me to let that dream go. I was crushed. I remember sitting on my bed in utter dismay. Could this be?

I have to be honest. My daughter took complete advantage of my low self-esteem. Of course she did. What kid wouldn't? I still doubted my authority over her, because I knew I was being trashed by her dad and her stepmom. I was trying so hard to avoid giving them ammunition that I didn't use all of my authority to parent my daughter. I didn't stand firm in my discipline, and when the teenage hormones kicked in, my world was once again rocked with words aimed straight at my heart: "I hate you!"

Though there are plenty of those kinds of stories, I also have memories of my daughter standing by my side when our church opened a new campus close to our home. In the days just before we opened our doors, we were asked to show up for one hour and read from the Bible. Caroline wanted to come with me for the reading. We both read, and it's a wonderful memory. I have no doubt, though, that if I had remarried during that time, I would more than likely not have had that memory and would probably have a second divorce under my belt!

Caroline's dad's side of the family had, and still have, a very condescending sense of humor. If you're degraded, then they're just "picking on you." It was how they showed what they called "love." With both of my kids, this sense of humor was impossible to break. Most of the time, Caroline and I were, and still are, very close, but her demeaning words and headstrong spirit would lay me flat. I know this is unacceptable as an excuse, and it's a lesson learned that I cannot undo. Caroline sees now, as a young mother herself, where I went wrong with her, and my prayer is that her marriage stays healthy and that I can advise her according to God's Word and not by how I actually handled a situation.

After reading this particular book, I had to sit back and honestly ask myself if I could bring a man into my life. I prayed and contemplated this for a few weeks. It was a very tough decision. Could I step away from the idea of marriage, which had always been my hope of being rescued, and instead lean on my only hope and trust in Him? Could I?

I finally admitted to myself that if I were to get married while Caroline lived at home, I was probably asking for trouble, and not because she was a bad kid. She tried my patience, and she made some bad choices, but she had my undivided attention. If I were to get married, I would have to put a husband first. Was I ready to do that? Could I make a choice between my child and a husband? The simple answer was no; I couldn't. The conclusion that I came to was that I couldn't get married while she lived at home. I would do the best I could to make sure our home was a good one, and I would be the best mother I could possibly be. And I would give up the idea of marriage for a few years.

There were many nights when I went to bed crying or praying in utter weariness for God to intervene in one of our fights. Did I make mistakes? Oh, yes, I did! But I know for sure that if I had dated someone and had actually made it to the wedding alter, I would have gone through another divorce. To this day, I have no doubts about that. There was no way I could have put my marriage first.

During this time, one of my favorite pastors taught a class on generational curses, and I realized that my mom had been sexually abused and that I had been sexually abused. I don't know the stories of my great-grandparents at all, but I've seen pictures. The eyes of my maternal great-grandmother are so sad, as are the eyes of my grandmother and my mother. It was time to stop the curse of sexual abuse. This class confirmed the decision that I had already made. No man was coming near my daughter. Period.

Am I telling you that you shouldn't get married if you have a teenage daughter? I wouldn't go that far, but at the same time I would highly advise you to pray and ask God what His desire is for you.

Another reason I delayed dating was because my daughter was absolutely gorgeous. I remember when she was thirteen and walking through a mall, and men turned to look, not at me but at her. She was all legs and long hair. She wore a size zero. She did a little modeling and knew how to carry herself. Did I want to enter a marriage, knowing how my stepdad had treated me? The possibility of accidental sightings of her in her bra and panties, or stepping out of a shower, or forgetting to close her bedroom door were huge. To this day I'm thankful that I waited to marry. And I'm thankful for that book! If it ever surfaces, and I find out who the author was, I will update this book to reflect that. I'd love to tell the author what a huge impact she made on my life.

Lesson Learned

"Trust in the LORD with all your heart and do not lean on your own understanding. In all your ways acknowledge Him, And He will make your paths straight" (Proverbs 3:5–6).

Learning to recognize God's voice through other Christians, especially their books, was such a gift! Stepping out in faith and making the decision not to marry while my daughter was home was a huge decision. But I wouldn't change a thing. I spent over seven years in my thirties and all of my forties as a divorced, single parent. That decision meant letting go of everything my flesh desired. But I grew spiritually! I grew enough to attract a strong, godly man (one *L*).

I was able to leave my desperation in my former life. There is freedom in Christ! Sisters, I pray that you find that freedom—and along with it, the joy and peace. There is nothing like it!

CHAPTER 7

Eyes on the Road: How to Stay Busy as a Single, Celibate, Christian Mother

Warning:
Not everyone who says to me, "Lord, Lord," will
enter the kingdom of heaven, but the one who does
the will of my Father who is in heaven.
— Matthew 7:21

Now that I've caught you up on where I went very wrong in almost every aspect of my life, I'd love to share with you how making *good* decisions brought great joy ... without a man!

I had always heard about volunteering, but I had never seen it demonstrated. My parents had lived their own twisted lives. My friends lived their own lives. So, what was this volunteering thing? What I learned was that it meant taking a chance. It meant hearing about a need and saying, "I can help!" It meant learning to incorporate one very simple but hard-to-say word in my vocabulary: *yes.*

I needed to do and learn things that were outside of my comfort zone. Once I joined a Bible study I was asked to be the social director. It was laughable, really. Me?

After all these years I had finally come to a point where I could go to a movie by myself and actually enjoy it. I enjoyed doing quite a lot of things by myself. I could eat at a restaurant, go for a walk, go to the zoo, take a drive, or spend the night at a hotel—and enjoy myself! What did I know about "social" anything?

But I had to ask myself if that was truly how I felt, or if I really feared the unknown. Did I fear that I might allow people in and they would start to ridicule me? Or maybe I was still worried about what Joey would say to our kids.

After praying and gathering my courage, I finally said yes, and what started out as a very scary thing actually turned in to a very liberating part of my life. I asked the director of our class, "What kinds of things should I plan?" His answer was awesome: "Whatever you want to do that will shine a light in the world and let people see that Christians can have fun without having to go to bars and drinking." Wow.

Besides going to the movies, I didn't know what Christian fun looked like. But this was a time when God was showing me how to get outside of myself, how to think outside the box and use my imagination. There I was in my forties, and this was a new concept for me!

So we went tubing down the Guadalupe. We went zip-lining. We went to the movies, and we had progressive dinners. We laughed together, and we prayed together. We rode paddleboats and splashed each other. I planned some trips that I couldn't afford to do myself, but that was okay. While others were going skiing in Colorado or scuba diving in the Caribbean, I was living my life and learning to smile and laugh. One night as I was contemplating my contentment, God reminded me that He had answered another prayer: "Lord, I just want to *laugh*!"

The more I learned to say yes, the more interesting my world became. I learned that there were needs that I had honestly learned to tune out because I figured someone else would do it.

But I learned to talk with my pastors, and more than one prayed with me and over me. As these fatherly men gave me the courage to step out into unknown territory, I actually volunteered at a homeless shelter and taught grown men English and math so they could pass their GEDsI, who had never gone to college! Who in the world would have thought I could do that? God did.

I listened to the advertisements on our local Christian radio station asking for volunteers at their concerts. I still loved music and had fallen in love with contemporary Christian music. So I said, "I can do that!" And I volunteered and went to concerts where people would come forward for prayer.

I went to seminars for singles, and I volunteered within my church to speak with people who came forward to accept Christ.

Then came the second lesson in volunteering: learning to say no! The ability to say no is also a necessity. When people realize that they can count on you, they can sometimes go to you because it's easier than finding someone else. It's really easy to take on too much. But when you're doing God's work and you're helping others—and still able to go to work and be a good parent—the rewards are amazing. The self-confidence that comes only from God and the assurance of the Holy Spirit can sky-rocket you to a whole new level of living.

Lesson Learned

"For you were called to freedom, brothers. Only do not use your freedom as an opportunity for the flesh, but through love serve one another. For the whole law is fulfilled in one word: "You shall love your neighbor as yourself" (Galatians 5:13–14).

This verse is so very true. (Aren't they all?) In learning to give to others, I was able to open my home to a couple of Caroline's friends and at least try to be a good influence on them. To this day, I'm still in contact with one of them, and she still calls me Mom.

In Rick Warren's book, *The Purpose Driven Life*, he talks about getting on a plane and praying for people and seeing an immediate reaction to the Holy Spirit as he watched their countenances lifted. I'm still learning to pray for others and put their needs above my own. It's not just a good idea. It's expected from His children!

CHAPTER 8

Glancing Back for Too Long: Sliding into the Ditch

Warning:
Be sober-minded; be watchful. Your adversary the devil prowls
around like a roaring lion, seeking someone to devour.
—1 Peter 5:8

This verse in 1 Peter was a wake-up call for me. I thought I had licked life! I was abstaining from sex. I wasn't dating. I had friends I could count on. I had a relationship with both of my children. My bills were being paid. What more could I ask? Sisters, you can never be too careful. We often hear sermons devoted to married couples on the dangers of complacency and the need to guard their marriages. Well, singles also need to guard their hearts and be careful of complacency.

I had found a godly rut for my life, and I thought nothing could pull me down. I had been abstaining from sex for almost seven years. I had been divorced for almost fourteen. Caroline was a freshman in a local junior college. I was *strong. I, me, myself*: those are dangerous words, especially for a single woman. We start thinking, "I am woman; hear me roar!" We've seen the evils of men, and we've learned to recognize the wolf in sheep's clothing. Or have we?

I found a well-known website for reuniting high school classmates. I started looking up people I used to know. It was so much fun! It was exciting to see how my high school friends had turned out. Almost all of them were still married to their first spouse. I was still struggling with admitting that I was divorced. But it was still good to catch up!

Then I found an old acquaintance, someone from a neighboring school on whom I had truly had a huge crush! Our parents had been friends back when we were in junior high. So of course I reached out, and we sent e-mails back and forth for almost a year. I was so proud of myself. I was keeping my distance. He had some red flags that I was definitely paying attention to. He was divorced but living in the same house as his ex-wife. They had an "arrangement." We lived about four hours apart, so I wasn't worried about growing attached. When Jack started calling me and I heard his voice for the first time in twenty-eight years, I have to admit that my heart did a little flip-flop. But I soon got it under control. After all, he still lived with the ex, and I wasn't going to get involved in *that*. He also had a four-year-old. I truly did not want to be a stepparent to a young child. I was almost through raising children! But what if this was from God? Would I still turn him away because I wanted to be selfish and not raise another child?

Well, one weekend he was in town attending a convention, and he asked if we could get together and maybe go dancing. I was very conflicted! I hadn't been on a date in years! But was this a date? No, it wasn't a date. It was just old friends getting together. Yes, okay, I could do that.

We met on a Sunday evening. We went to a local dance hall, and sure enough, he was an awesome dancer. He was also a smooth talker, which I recognized. But the dancing was such fun after not dancing for so long. We danced for hours and talked and caught up on each other's lives. I had forgotten what it felt like to be held by a man, and how powerful it was to be moving in unison to the music.

I explained to him that I wasn't going to have sex outside of marriage, and he was very comfortable with that, which made my heart soar! His first marriage had supposedly been a godly courtship, so he said he understood.

As we caught up, I learned that he had gone to school to become a Baptist pastor but hadn't finished. He was now a businessman and loved his job. He had a secondary income coming in from some family oil wells. I was just so impressed with everything about him. That night he kissed me on the cheek and asked if he could call me again sometime. Of course I said yes. And of course I felt like I was walking on air the next day!

Ladies, I know Satan used every one of my old "triggers" to send me back to my old ways. Jack moved out of his wife's home and decided to go back to school and finish his degree. His college of choice was almost exactly halfway between his daughter and me.

At first he would drive up to see his daughter on one weekend (presumably staying in a hotel), and the next weekend he would stay in a hotel near me.

However, within six months we were sexually involved, and I was heading toward another heartbreak. I cannot describe the feeling of self-loathing, disappointment, anger, humiliation, regret, and deep sorrow I felt after the first time we were together.

Once again, sex had blinded me to a man's faults. It took several months before I realized that he was a functional alcoholic, which means that he could have a few drinks and still have the appearance of being completely sober. And more gut-wrenching than that, I found out that he was still sleeping with his ex-wife. (I know you saw that one coming, right?)

But this time, instead of calling in sick to work, locking myself in my bedroom, not eating, and feeling sorry for myself, I stood up to this man who had stolen the heart I had guarded for so long. I looked him in the eye and told him exactly what I thought. Then I drove home, looked at myself in the mirror, and tried to see where I had gone wrong.

I realized that I had started thinking that I was invincible instead of relying 100 percent on an invincible God. When you take Him out of the relationship, you *will* fall. The one thing different about this heartbreak, though, was knowing I could ask for forgiveness. And I did, on bended knee. I was ashamed. I was contrite, and I was heavyhearted. But God reached down and reminded me that I was forgiven. I can't begin to describe to you the joy that came to me as I reveled in His forgiveness! And I can't begin to explain the depth of my determination to hold on to my Lord and Savior and never let go!

I had stepped away from the church during this time, and I decided to go back to just the worship service. I really didn't want to be involved in a singles Bible study at that time. Most people knew me, and they knew my views on celibacy, and I just couldn't admit my failure.

I curtailed my volunteer activities within the church and concentrated on work. I was still volunteering for the Christian radio station and doing a few other things. I had also found a class to become a certified Christian counselor. I dove into that class. Though my shame was deeper after this relationship, my grief was not as deep as in previous breakups. I now had my Lord and Savior in my corner, and I felt His forgiveness in such a way that I knew I had learned a very valuable lesson.

Lesson Learned

"If we confess our sins, he is faithful and just to forgive us [our] sins, and to cleanse us from all unrighteousness" (1 John 1:9).

I pray that each of you can learn to lean on Jesus, to trust Him as your husband, and to accept His forgiveness. Have you seen the movie *The Passion of the Christ*? That movie didn't go anywhere near to the true depth of Christ's suffering for you, for me, for the world. What more can I say? Can you imagine a love any deeper than that? His forgiveness is for all, even for me in my mistakes, even for you. It's a gift. In order for a gift to be given, it must be received. I pray that you decide to receive what is already yours!

CHAPTER 9

Eyes on the Road:
Ways God Came Through for Me

Warning:
And he said to them, "Why are you afraid, O you of little faith?"
— Matthew 8:26

In Hebrews 11, we are given a definition of faith: "Now faith is the substance of things hoped for, the evidence of things not seen."

During my time as a single Christian, especially when I first came to Christ, God came through for me in so many ways. I used to think He was actually showing off for me. He is an amazing God. He is *the* Alpha and *the* Omega, and yet He knows every hair on my head. He had nothing to prove to me, but He still amazed me. He still showed up. I'd like to tell you of some of the places in my life where He truly came through for me in a tangible way. I've held on to these moments in times of weakness and doubt.

I Should Have Died

One morning, just a week after my "nose-to-the-carpet" night, I was driving to work and came to a four-way stop at which I stopped every morning. But on this particular morning, my heart was light, and there was a song on my lips for Him. I was truly *delighting* myself in Him.

I came up to the stop sign and stopped. I looked left and then right, and there were no cars in sight. I pulled into the intersection and just as I was half-way through it, I saw on my left side a car that must have flown through the stop sign. I could see the front of his car, for his headlights were only a few feet away from the driver's side door. I knew I was about to die.

He was too close for me to get out of his way. I pushed my foot on the gas, knowing that it was futile. And then the strangest thing happened. It was as if there was some type of time warp. It's the only way I can even attempt to explain it.

I should have been hit. But I blinked, and I and my car were on the other side of the intersection, untouched. The other car had hit his brakes, but had also made it through the intersection. I was pretty shaken, but that was my first experience with what must have been angels looking out for me. I've told this story many times and am constantly amazed at the stories that I've been told in return.

God Gave Me Strength

I previously told you about the attic leak. I had another experience in the attic that wasn't as traumatic, but I'll never forget it. My air conditioning duct was leaking cold air straight into the attic. I had tried to fix it with duct tape, but it wasn't holding very well, so I went to the hardware store and bought some ducting. How hard could it be? I bought some wire cutters and began pulling the ducting out of the box. Getting it tied and taped around the first AC opening was easy, but cutting the end of it? I couldn't do it. The wire cutters weren't sharp enough (or maybe I just wasn't strong enough).

It was June, and it was Texas, and the attic was very stuffy. I ran back to the hardware store and bought a larger set of wire cutters. I got home and still couldn't cut through the wire. I had to get it fixed before Caroline came home, or we wouldn't be able to sleep that night. It was just way too hot!

There are times when single women can really get disheartened, and there are times when Satan knows that he can work on us. This was one of those times. I was sweaty and hot and miserable, and all I wanted was a man's strength to cut through the stupid wire so that I could turn the AC back on. It was such a simple thing! By this time in my life, my son had completely stopped talking to me, so I couldn't call him, and I didn't feel comfortable calling a man in the church. I had seen too many women acting helpless and getting a man to come over—and then actually pursuing the poor guy. I didn't want anyone thinking I was helpless or that I had designs on anyone.

I started crying, and then I sat up straight and said, "I *can* do all things through Christ who strengthens me!" *Squeeze.* "I can *do* all things through Christ who strengthens me!" *Squeeze.* "I can do *all* things ..." *Squeeze. Snap!* The wire was cut, and I was able to finish. Hallelujah! Through that simple act and that simple prayer of faith, He showed up. It's a small thing, but when you start seeing God in the small stuff, you know to expect Him in the big stuff.

Meeting Mr. Right!

There were many, many instances when God came through for me, but this is one of the best stories I have. It takes all my heartaches, sorrows, and lessons learned and brings them to fruition—not that marriage should be a "goal." Our goal should be to please God and to reach others for Christ. If He knows that you can be equally yoked and reach more people, then He'll allow that to happen. I truly believe this!

After being out of a singles' Bible study for a few years, I decided it was time to go back. I called a friend and said, "Tell me about your Bible study."

"Well," she said, "it's supposed to be for people in their forties, but most of the people are older, in their late fifties or early sixties."

"That's okay," I responded. "I'm fifty, so I'm right in the middle."

Maria plunged ahead and said, "And I'm the evangelism director, but I'm about to get married. I think you'd be perfect for the job."

Now, my friend Maria has this "tone" she uses when she sounds like she's teasing, but you know you're about to do exactly what she's asking of you. I knew that tone. I tried to back down, but she was hearing none of it. I conceded and went to her Bible study that weekend.

The class had just had a change in leadership, and the new director was getting his sea legs under him. Maria grabbed me, took me over to Ken, and let him know that I would be the perfect replacement when she left. We shook hands, and I had to pull my head back to look him in the eye. I was five foot five, and he had to be around six foot two!

However, I never gave him a second glance or even a second thought, if I'm going to be honest. I truly wasn't interested in dating again. I didn't trust myself, and I wasn't about to chance a relationship in the church where I'd seen others humiliated when relationships hadn't worked out. I didn't believe in online dating, I didn't believe in long-distance dating, I didn't believe in being unequally yoked, and I didn't believe in dating in the church. I'm not sure how I thought I was ever to get married again, but after nineteen years, I had seriously given up. Now Ken will tell you a very different story of how I would look for him when I walked into the classroom and smile. Others would nudge him and tell him that I kept looking at him. No. That is not my memory at all!

Others will say they knew we'd end up together the first time they saw us at a class social. They may have known, but I have to say that God was keeping me in the dark on that one!

When did it dawn on me that he might actually be a suitable suitor? When he said, "I love that the singles in this church are pursuing godly relationships and refraining from sex."

I almost choked on the food I was eating at that moment. Such naïveté! I was conflicted on how to burst his bubble.

He must have seen the look on my face, because he questioned me. "They are, aren't they?"

I sighed and said, "No, they're not. Some of them are, but most of them are not." He was absolutely astounded, and I found myself drawn to that. I felt my heart get just a little bit soft. But I was guarding it!

I'd love to share some of the things that made our courtship different from the average fifty-something-year-olds. (He's actually three and a half years younger than I am, so he was still in his forties).

Courting Lessons 101

1. *We did not engage in sex.* Yes, that's a given, but how do you do that? Most couples are spending the nights at each other's homes and becoming a fixture in the lives of the each other's kids. Ken had two teenage boys, and we both wanted to be examples of a godly courtship. I was an empty-nester, so it wasn't such a big deal for me. So we did not spend the night at each other's homes. (It did help that we only lived five miles from each other.)

    Since I *was* an empty-nester, it would have been very easy for my house to become the place where we consummated our love for each other, but we made it a rule to try not to be there alone with each other. We did watch an occasional movie there, but it was pretty rare. Instead we went out to eat—a lot.

2. *We served together* in a couple of ministries. One of the things that is so important here is that the ministries just happened to coincide with our gifts. We found ourselves serving together. Neither of us went out of way to manipulate where we volunteered. We weren't changing who we were to try to pursue the other person. Serving together gives you a peek into the other person's

sense of commitment. What are his gifts? Is he compassionate, giving, and forgiving?

This gave us a knowledge of each other that we would not have been able to obtain in any other way.

3. *We spent Sundays together.* Sometimes he would pick me up for church, and sometimes I would meet him there. Afterward, we would meet with our singles class for lunch. And after that? Many times we would go to a bookstore and buy a book full of questions about relationships. We tried to make sure they were written by Christian authors, and usually they were. (If they weren't, we skipped over the questions that assumed we were sexually involved.) We would sit and have a cup of coffee and ask each other questions. This could take hours! There were times when it was so interesting that we would continue the conversation over the phone that night, each reading a question to the other, and both of us having to answer.

I have to warn you that there were times when answering the questions or hearing the answers was really, really tough. Bearing in mind that his wife had cheated on him and that his breakup was much fresher than mine, we had different perspectives on various things. But it was really good that we sorted through a lot of muck before we were married. This simple little thing was *huge* in building our knowledge of each other. You see, because sex was "off the table," it forced us to talk and get to know each other on a whole different level. This was new for both of us.

4. *We did not pray together.* Whoa! In Ben Young's book, *The Ten Commandments of Dating*, he writes, "Praying is one of the most intimate experiences you can ever have. Consider the fact that when you pray with someone you hardly know, you are encouraging a bond that can be more intense than even physical affection or sex. There is a fine line between spirituality and

97

sexuality, and people who do not respect that line are in danger of getting burned."

Yes, Ken prayed before our meals, but our first prayer together as a couple was on our wedding night.

After a year of friendship, with the last six months being a time of dating, it became apparent that we were heading toward marriage. While we both agree that we probably should have dated another six months, I think God had a hand in things when I was laid off from my job a couple of weeks before Thanksgiving. We had a choice. I could start looking for another job, knowing that Ken would truly love having me be a stay-at-home wife, or we could move things up a bit. I know that he prayed about it, and I of course was praying about our next steps.

Well, I enjoyed an absolutely beautiful proposal. It involved my friends, my family, a limo, and a private room in a very nice restaurant. He asked me to marry him, and I said yes. We decided to marry between Christmas and New Year's. Caroline had moved to Las Vegas, and we found ourselves planning a small ceremony at a chapel there. The ceremony was really beautiful. The pastor had me in tears.

I'll never forget my future son-in-law's words as we were waiting on the pastor: "Shh! Do you hear that?" We all stopped and listened. I know I must have looked totally bewildered. "That's the sound of nobody stressing out!" It gave us all a good chuckle because we knew he was hinting at a small wedding also. (It didn't work.) We honeymooned in Hawaii. It was truly romantic and more than I had ever dreamed of.

God showed up on that honeymoon too. He knew I'd had a vision of what my "dream" wedding night would be. I would be the nervous bride in the bathroom. (I was terrified!) I would wear a long white gown to present myself to my husband. He wouldn't tear my clothes off, but he would grab my hand, lead me to the side of the bed, and ask for God's blessing on our union. And that was exactly what happened. It was absolutely one of the most "unifying" prayers that I had ever prayed.

I'm not going to say that our first year was all peaches and cream. Ken likens it to the taming of a wild mare (me). He'd only been divorced for a short time when we started dating, while I had been single and had already gone through the empty-nest syndrome. He had two teenage boys still at home. My daughter was living her life in another state, and my son hadn't talked to me in almost seven years by this time. My world had once again been turned completely upside down.

But I went into the marriage knowing that it would take some work. Marriage means commitment. It means trying and trying and trying. After one particularly bad argument, I was truly just wanting to leave. Inside I was screaming to the Lord and asking for grace and patience and, most of all, wisdom. We were both overwhelmed and believing that we had made a mistake (which is pretty common for the first year of a second marriage, I found out). But I looked him straight in the eye and said, "Well, there's no back door. Now what?"

It was a turning point, because we both realized to a deeper degree that this was forever. Love is easy, but marriage can be hard at times. It's a decision to stick to the covenant, God's covenant, and to make it work. We both made that decision, and it's working.

As of the writing of this last chapter, we've been married almost six years, and I'm now a grandmother to four grandchildren! My son and I have salvaged something of a relationship, and my daughter lives close enough to have lunch with me sometimes, and then I can grab some awesome hugs from the grandbabies. I'm blessed that they can spend the night and that they love Ken.

I'm not going to make a promise that God will show up for you in your life in the exact same way He did for me. He doesn't work like that. What I can promise you is that if you stop looking in the rearview mirror, keep your life moving forward, lift your eyes up to Him, and acknowledge Him as your holy God, your husband, your Father, your shoulder, your lifesaver, and your all in all, your life will take on meaning. You *will* find that elusive thing called contentment.

I'm not even going to promise you that you'll find Mr. Right. If that's God's will for your life, then I pray that you do! But I *can* promise that He will be there for you. Look for Him in the small things, and He'll be there in the big things!

"And Jesus answered them, 'Truly, I say to you, if you have faith and do not doubt, you will not only do what has been done to the fig tree, but even if you say to this mountain, "Be taken up and thrown into the sea," it will happen. And whatever you ask in prayer, you will receive, if you have faith'" (Matthew 21:21–22).

Above all, pray for God's will to be done in your life. His ways are not our ways (Isaiah 55:8). His way may be down a path that you will truly not understand. But hold on, sister. Hold on.

And remember that you are a princess! Romans 8:16–17 says, "The Spirit Himself testifies with our spirit that we are children of God, and if children, heirs also, heirs of God and fellow heirs with Christ." Did you read that? We are heirs with Christ. That makes you a princess. Walk with your head up and shoulders back, content and joyful in the knowledge that you are loved so much!

May God be with you and bless you ever so abundantly!

CPSIA information can be obtained
at www.ICGtesting.com
Printed in the USA
BVHW030213130521
607257BV00006B/96

9 781512 729672